# IN DEFENSE OF THE GOSPELS

## THE GOSPELS

*The Case for Reliability*

Rom. 8:28

# IN DEFENSE OF THE GOSPELS

*The Case for Reliability*

## JOHN STEWART

INTELLIGENT FAITH PRESS

**In Defense of the Gospels**
*The Case for Reliability*

© 2018 By John Stewart

Published by Intelligent Faith Press
P.O. Box 186, Panora, Iowa 50216
www.IntelligentFaith.com

# CONTENTS

# ACKNOWLEDGMENTS

My interest in the Bible in general and the Gospels in particular has been stoked by several people. As a new believer in 1970 I attended a Monday night Bible class taught by the well-known radio Bible teacher J. Vernon McGee. My brother and I waited around after the class to ask questions, and to our delight he graciously answered them. I later attended college where I greatly benefitted from Bible survey courses taught by Curtis Mitchell who had been one of McGee's students. These two created a strong desire in me to learn everything I could about the Scriptures. Another college professor who had a profound influence was Harry Sturz, an expert in New Testament textual criticism who was instrumental in my decision to write my master's thesis on a textual problem found in John 3:13.

On a parallel track with my interest in the Bible was my passion for learning the evidence that supports the truth of Christianity (the field of "Christian Apologetics"). As a new believer I was enthralled by talks from popular apologist Josh McDowell and the writings of Church historian John Warwick Montgomery. Around the same time I attended a series on the cults taught by Walter Martin, the leading expert on the cults, whose style inspired me to boldly proclaim the truth of the Gospel. These three profoundly shaped my thinking. Perhaps it was providential that they eventually became friends and colleagues—Josh ending up co-writing several books with my brother Don, Montgomery chose me to be a charter faculty member of the first school to offer a graduate level degree in apologetics (Simon Greenleaf School of Law) and Walter Martin brought me in as his first co-host of his nationally-syndicated radio show the *Bible Answerman*.

After more than four decades studying the Bible and apologetics I felt the urge to pass on what I had discovered over the years. Thus, when considering all the topics that seemed important to write about, one stood out as pre-eminent—the reliability of the Gospels. The more I thought about it, nothing seemed as important as the issue of whether the Gospels are true accounts of the life and teachings of Jesus. I then began the lengthy process of developing an approach to presenting evidence for the Gospels' reliability. From my experience as a trial lawyer and Christian apologist I began organizing material as if I were presenting a case in court. There were several issues that had to be addressed to properly make a case for whether the Gospels are trustworthy, and these issues became the six questions I address in this book *In Defense of the Gospels*.

Several people deserve a special mention for making this book possible. First is my wife Laurie, whose encouragement helped me through the countless hours of research and writing. Next is my editor Scott Stewart, whose eye for detail is amazing. It was providential to find Scott, an evangelical who is a great editor and theologically savvy. Additionally, I am indebted to author James Agresti who graciously agreed to read my manuscript. Jim made many helpful suggestions that are incorporated into the book. Finally, the way I address issues in the book was gleaned from the work of several top evangelical scholars, including Gary Habermas, Craig Evans and Craig Blomberg. To these men I owe a debt of gratitude.

Last, a special thanks to all the people whose kind words, prayers and support have enabled Laurie and me to engage in an international speaking, teaching and training ministry for more than a decade. Our ministry, now called "Intelligent Faith" (www.IntelligentFaith.com), partners with Ratio Christi ("Reason of Christ" in Latin), a student-faculty apologetic alliance, to bring evidence for the truth of Christianity to the world. I previously served as Executive Director for Ratio Christi International and now am Ratio Christi's Scholar in Residence. My blogs appear on the Intelligent Faith website and at JohnMarkStewart. blogspot.com. *Sola deo Gloria* ("to God alone be the glory")!

# PREFACE

## WHAT PROMPTED THIS BOOK?

Many books have been written about the New Testament Gospels, from primers for beginners to scholarly works for experts in the field. My interest in the Gospels goes back four decades, to a time when I first wanted to know more than *what* they said--I wanted to know whether the accounts in the Gospels were *true*. I began formally studying the historical reliability of the Gospels, and along the way earned a bachelor's degree in biblical studies and a master's in theological studies. After that I set out to understand the nature and use of evidence because I wanted to test my conclusions about the Gospels and Christianity by means of logic, reason and legal standards of proof. That goal led me to law school where I earned a doctorate in jurisprudence. I became a lawyer and law school professor, and have taught college and graduate level courses on the evidence and reasons why Christianity is true (the field of "Christian apologetics").

In the past decade I've had many opportunities to talk about the historical reliability of the Gospels to a broad range of people in America, Africa, Asia and Europe, speaking at universities, churches, conferences, and even formally teaching doctoral students. My interactions with these groups made it clear that there was a lack of easily digestible information about the Gospels. Few people knew the evidence supporting the reliability of the Gospels, and even fewer could defend the Gospels against common objections. As I surveyed available literature on the subject, I found plenty of books and articles skeptical of the historical reliability of the Gospels, but relatively few answered the skeptics.

The time was right to respond to critics in a straightforward manner to help students, parents, Bible schools, seminaries, churches, and lay people. Thus *In Defense of the Gospels* was born.

This book is intended for readers of all levels. It is simple enough for beginners to understand the arguments and evidence presented, but sufficiently deep for more erudite readers. But before jumping in to the arguments and evidence, I want to address the question of how critical attacks on the Gospels and Christianity ever became so prominent in our culture, prompting *In Defense of the Gospels*.

## THE RISE OF A NEW SKEPTICISM

Since the 1st century the Gospels of Matthew, Mark, Luke, and John have been virtually the sole sources of information about the life and teachings of Jesus. Few questioned the reliability of the Gospel accounts until about 200 years ago, when "critical" schools in Germany began doubting certain aspects of the biblical accounts. What started as scholarly skepticism slowly grew into an entire cottage industry of questioning everything about Jesus, including whether He even existed. Until the 1960s, however, the arguments of skeptics of Christianity were confined to a few liberal seminaries and graduate schools, and atheism was largely seen as a "fringe" position, unworthy of devoting significant time and attention to refute it.

By the late 1960s secular intellectuals attempted to bring liberal and skeptical views of Christianity into mainstream America. It was a time when opposition to the Vietnam War brought about a counter-culture movement that eschewed traditional views, values and practices. Rock & roll music, drugs, hippies, "free love" and cultural iconoclasm threatened to take America's youth in a new direction, one that abandoned all vestiges of the "establishment," including America's dominant religion—Christianity. Hoping to ride the swell of irreligion, in 1969 atheist philosopher Paul Kurtz founded Prometheus Books as a publishing vehicle for atheists and skeptics. In 1972 Kurtz wrote his own book, *The New Skepticism,* and labeled his approach to finding truth "skeptical inquiry," a euphemism for anti-supernaturalism, and a guiding principle of secularism.

Despite a growing secularism, America was not yet ready to surrender its religious traditions. As Prometheus Books was churning out attacks on religion, a movement of young people who found a new interest in biblical Christianity sprang up largely from outside the traditional church, dubbed the "Jesus Movement." The early 1970s saw the rise of independent churches, "contemporary Christian music," informal worship services, a "charismatic renewal" within mainline Protestant denominations, fascination with Bible prophecy, and a renewed emphasis on studying the Bible. Current events were read alongside passages from the Bible, as Hal Lindsay's 1970 bestseller *The Late, Great Planet Earth* linked global events with end-time Bible prophecies.

As secularism continued encroaching on Christian culture, in 1972 Josh McDowell penned the first popular book presenting evidence in defense of Christianity, *Evidence That Demands a Verdict.* While McDowell's book convinced many that Christianity was intellectually defensible, secularism continued to infiltrate universities in the early 1970s, and was poised to become dominant in American culture. At a time when Christian thinkers had an opportunity to vigorously address the skeptical challenges to Christianity that accompany secularism, many retreated instead into a debate over whether the Bible was inerrant. While evangelicals and mainline Protestants squared off against each other as chronicled in Harold Lindsell's 1976 book *The Battle for the Bible*, agnostics and atheists doubled down on efforts to take skepticism mainstream.

The challenges to Christianity did motivate some Christian thinkers into action. In 1980 theologian and historian John Warwick Montgomery founded the Simon Greenleaf School of Law, which offered the first ever master's degree in Christian Apologetics. Montgomery's prescience was followed by theologian Francis Schaeffer's 1981 book, *A Christian Manifesto,* that outlined both the crisis of a pervasive secularism and the need for Christians to re-engage and reclaim the culture. Unfortunately, the church at large seemed unaware that Christianity's cultural dominance was waning. Seminaries seemed disinterested in training students to defend Christianity against secular attacks, leaving future church leaders without the awareness, training and techniques necessary to properly address the new skepticism.

The secularists first garnered the attention of evangelicals on a large scale in the mid-1980s when a self-appointed group of liberal scholars called the "Jesus Seminar" had the temerity to vote on whether Jesus' words in the Gospels were authentic. They concluded that fewer than 20 percent of the words attributed to Jesus originated with Him. The unorthodox findings of the Jesus Seminar made world headlines, and this was the general population's first exposure to the claim that the Gospels were not historically reliable. Skepticism had now gone mainstream.

Evangelical scholars viewed the Jesus Seminar with jaundiced eyes, noting that the 150 Jesus Seminar scholars were all from the liberal side of Christianity whose conclusions were nothing new. But the protestations of Bible-believing Christians were drowned out by a new interest in scholarly skepticism toward Christianity that had suddenly become newsworthy. Mainstream media realized that the Jesus Seminar's sensational claims created a buzz that drew people in, creating a hunger for more. This hunger became an invitation for more liberal scholars and popular writers to offer anti-Christian polemics, resulting in new and more sensational claims from skeptics. This was a harbinger of what was to come.

The classical atheism of the 1960s and 1970s never went mainstream despite the best efforts of writers such as Bertrand Russell, George Smith and Anthony Flew. Though their philosophical approach to atheism was unable to make inroads into the cultural psyche, a new flavor of atheism was about to emerge--"scientific atheism." America and Britain were ready to lap it up. In 1986, British biologist Richard Dawkins wrote *The Blind Watchmaker,* which established him as a spokesperson for both atheism and anti-Christian polemics. The perfect storm of a rising secularism, the Jesus Seminar and Richard Dawkins opened a door of opportunity for the new genre of scholarly skepticism, and through that door stepped theologian and textual critic Bart Ehrman.

In the 1990s Ehrman, a former fundamentalist Christian turned "agnostic atheist," began writing popular books questioning the foundational tenets of Christianity. His provocative titles helped launch five of his books onto the New York Times bestseller list, making Ehrman the champion of those who wanted reasons to reject the evangelical version of Christianity. In works such as *The Orthodox Corruption of Scripture* (1996), *Misquoting Jesus* (2005) and *Jesus Interrupted* (2009), Ehrman engaged in a frontal attack on the reliability of the Bible, as seen in his subtitles: *Revealing the Hidden Contradictions in the Bible (And Why We Don't Know About Them)* and *The Story Behind Who Changed the Bible and Why.* Twenty-five years earlier Ehman's books would have drawn a yawn and remained virtually unnoticed except in academia. But by the 1990s conditions were just right for him to emerge as the point man for scholarly skepticism of Christianity.

## THE BRAVE NEW SECULAR WORLD

Bart Ehrman's popular critiques of the New Testament were accompanied by the advent of a newer and bolder form of atheism. Traditional atheism was replaced by anti-theists who did not merely disbelieve in God, but despised the idea of the traditional God of Judaism and Christianity. In his 2006 bestseller Richard Dawkins calls belief in God a "delusion" (*The God Delusion*). Dawkins was part of a trinity of popular anti-theist writers that included the late Christopher Hitchens (*God is Not Great: How Religion Poisons Everything*, 2007) and Sam Harris (*The End of Faith: Religion, Terror and the Future of Reason*, 2004).

Fiction writer Dan Brown's 2003 novel *The Da Vinci Code* added fuel to the fire of skepticism. The story attacks the reliability of the Gospel accounts of Jesus at nearly every turn and presents as true the shocking revelation that Jesus was married to Mary Magdalene who bore His child. Brown's novel became a literary *tours de force*, selling more than 80 million copies. Despite a number of books and articles written to refute Brown's claims, many people who read *The Da Vinci Code* were left with the impression that the story of Jesus is so entrenched in murky traditions that it is impossible to know the truth. The cumulative effect of the Jesus Seminar and the writings of Ehrman, et al., created a paradigm shift in how many viewed the Gospels. The new default setting was skepticism, a sea change from past generations that assumed the Gospels were completely true and historically reliable.

## THE GOOD NEWS

The new skepticism has awakened a sleeping giant of Christians who recognize, for the most part, that universities and mainstream media have not fairly presented the "other side" of the debate, namely evidence that supports Christianity. Attacks on Christianity, in general, and especially the Gospels, have been a catalyst for fueling a renaissance in Christian thinking, writing and advocacy. While some prefer to circle the wagons or add another layer to the wall that insulates believer from unbeliever, a new generation of thinking Christians has been motivated by the Scriptural command to "be ready to make a defense" for having hope in Jesus (1 Peter 3:15). This has brought about a renewed interest in Christian Apologetics and a host of books, articles, "intelligent faith" conferences, and formal study. Even churches that historically avoided polemics have begun to realize that 21st century people increasingly want to know *why* they should believe.

## A FINAL WORD

My goal in this book is to set forth the evidence for the historical reliability of the Gospels in a simple, straightforward manner. I address the six main issues people commonly raise concerning the Gospels, presenting each issue simply and succinctly, followed by the argument and the points of evidence that support the Gospels. The heart of each chapter is an expansion of the argument and evidence. I discuss most technical matters in endnotes, which provide explanations and resources for those who wish to look deeper into related issues.

Although I have made efforts to present skeptical views accurately, my aim in this book is not to make readers experts in critical views but rather to make the reader *aware* of skeptical views and provide evidence that counters those views.

If you are a college student who has never been exposed to evidence that supports the Gospels as historically reliable, this book might provide sufficient facts and arguments to prevent a crisis of faith that often occurs when first confronted with skeptics' challenges.

If you are the parents of a young person, this book provides a factual, evidence-based argument you can share with youth who need to know *why* they should believe the story of Jesus.

If you are a skeptic, even if all your questions are not resolved favorably toward Christianity, letting the evidence lead where it will might just lead you to recognize that Christianity has answers—even *good* answers—to the skeptical challenges to the Gospels.

Finally, whether you are already convinced the Gospels are reliable, or are taking a second look at the accounts of Jesus after questioning their accuracy, I encourage you to follow the evidence. May we all know the truth so that the truth can make us free.

# INTRODUCTION
# Gospels: The Foundation
# of Christianity

"...and you will know the truth, and the truth will make you free." John 8:32

## WHY IT MATTERS IF THE GOSPELS ARE TRUE

Christianity stands or falls on the truth of a bold claim, namely that the Creator revealed Himself and His plan for humanity through Jesus of Nazareth. The life and teachings of Jesus are presented in the first four books of the New Testament, called the "Gospels." Christianity contends the Gospels are reliable records of Jesus' life and teachings, and therefore can be trusted to present the truth about God's plan for all people. Skeptics question the historical reliability of the Gospels. If the Gospel accounts are not reliable, then all of Christianity's claims are suspect, at best, and false, at worst. Without evidence to support its claims, Christianity is merely one of many human attempts to make sense of our existence, relying on traditions, wish projection and blind faith rather than evidence. If evidence supports the reliability of the Gospels accounts, there is a factual basis for accepting Christianity's unique and exclusive claims as true.

How important is it to establish, one way or another, whether the message of the Gospels is true? Christian apologist and one-time atheist C. S. Lewis eloquently framed the issue this way:

> One must keep on pointing out that Christianity is a statement which, if false, is of *no* importance, and, if true, of infinite importance. The only thing it cannot be is moderately important.[1]

## WHAT ARE THE "GOSPELS"?

The word "gospel" means "good news." The term "Gospels" historically refers to Matthew, Mark, Luke, and John, the first four books of the New Testament in the Bible. These books focus on the life and teachings of Jesus of Nazareth. Before the 20th century, with very few exceptions, the content and claims of the Gospels were held to be absolutely true. Western culture used the term "gospel" from the 13th century onward to describe something as true as the biblical Gospels (e.g., "I saw Jack and Jill holding hands--that's gospel."). By the 17th century cultural respect for the reliability of the Gospels lead to the creation of the term "gospel truth," meaning something that is undeniably true. This expression shows "Gospel" and "truth" were considered synonymous, leading to a related expression "accept it as gospel," meaning "regarding it as being absolutely true."

These positive expressions about the Gospels gradually fell out of common usage with the advent of critical scrutiny of the Bible in the 18th century along with the continued rise of secularism in the West and the resulting decline in biblical literacy. The Gospels no longer enjoyed a favored status as they once did. In our day, they are a mystery to many, often seen only through the lens of popular writers who question, compare and disparage the Gospels.

In an age when audiences welcome new and different ideas, especially those that attack traditions and previously "off limits" topics, the Gospels have become a popular target for criticism. Attacks on the Gospels have left many people bewildered, torn between not wanting to abandon their religious traditions drawn from the Gospels and not wanting to appear gullible or uninformed when someone raises questions about their reliability.

The intent of this book is to equip readers with sufficient evidence to speak knowledgeably, with summarized and fully documented arguments, on questions of Gospel reliability.

## APPROACHING THE QUESTION OF THE GOSPELS' HISTORICAL RELIABILITY

### WEIGHING THE EVIDENCE

Do the Gospels deserve the high regard in which they were once held? There is no debate about the profound influence the Gospels have had on the world, particularly on the West, but they no longer hold sway as they once did. Is the diminished cultural relevance of the Gospels a result of their being weighed in the balance of history and found wanting, or is it due to misconceptions about their nature and reliability, biblical illiteracy, pseudo-skepticism or a secular agenda? These questions are best be answered by appealing to the evidence.

Regardless of how we got to this place, it is time to take a fresh look at the Gospels and consider evidence that addresses the question of whether they are reliable historical documents. If evidence shows the Gospels are, indeed, merely the accumulation of oral traditions and religious folklore divorced from actual history, then they may deserve to be demoted to the status of literary fiction, similar to *Gulliver's Travels*. However, if the weight of the evidence supports the historical reliability of the Gospel accounts, then a thinking person would do well to investigate the Gospels' claims and the answers they provide for humanity's ultimate questions.

## AVOIDING THE EXTREMES

In approaching the evidence relevant to the question of the Gospels' historical reliability, there are two extremes. First is *uncritical gullibility*. This extreme usually involves believers who equate any quest for evidence with doubt or unbelief. They treat questioning the conclusions of church leaders believed to be "men of God" as virtually questioning God Himself. Ancient wisdom rejects this extreme, asserting, "the simple believe anything, but the prudent give thought to their steps" (Proverbs 14:15).

Those who accept everything they are told without question may still be embracing the truth, provided what they are told comports with the evidence. However, there is little chance that such people will be able to obey the Scriptural command to "be ready to make a defense of the hope that is in you" (1 Peter 3:15), an admonition for believers to know and be ready to explain *why* they believe the Christian message.

In contrast, in an increasingly secular age, a new *critical gullibility* has arisen. This extreme accepts anything that is skeptical of historic Christianity, regardless of how unsupported or nonsensical the criticism. As New Testament scholar Craig Evans points out, "Some scholars seem to think that the more skeptical they are, the more critical they are…a lot of what passes for criticism is not critical at all; it is nothing more than skepticism masquerading as scholarship."[2] Much of the professed skepticism today is more accurately understood as *pseudo-skepticism,* where truth is subordinated to the desire to refute Christian beliefs.

Both uncritical gullibility and critical gullibility are obstacles in assessing the data to arrive at conclusions based on evidence and reason. It may be futile to encourage people, whether believer or skeptic, to "have an open mind." But even people who approach issues with extreme biases will sometimes change their views when confronted with compelling evidence. Therefore, I challenge all seekers of truth--whether Christian or skeptic, believer or doubter--to let the evidence answer the question of whether the Gospels tell us the truth about the life and teachings of Jesus.

## DETERMINING THE RELIABILITY OF THE GOSPELS

Serious historians acknowledge that historical knowledge only deals with degrees of probability and never with certainty.[3] Not having though *absolute* certainty, however, does not preclude the historian from having *adequate* certainty.[4] Careful historians employ such terms as "highly probable" or "highly improbable" when addressing whether events occurred as set forth in ancient documents. To determine the probability that the Gospels are reliable history, we must address six questions that have a direct bearing on their reliability. These six questions represent the most common challenges to the Gospels, and we will address each in a separate chapter in this book. The questions are:

1. *Were the Gospels written close enough in time to the life of Jesus that eyewitnesses were still alive who could reasonably remember the events and teachings?*

If the Gospels were written when eyewitnesses were still alive, then the Gospels may have been written by eyewitnesses or by those who received their information from eyewitnesses. Also, if the Gospels were written while eyewitnesses were still alive, then hostile witnesses would also be alive. The lack of criticism of the Gospel accounts from any 1st century sources would then carry some weight as an argument for reliability. Thus the issue of when the Gospels were written is relevant to the question of their reliability, and the issue of when they were written should be decided based on direct and circumstantial evidence.

*2. Were the Gospel writers either eyewitnesses or recorders of the accounts of eyewitnesses?*

Although many historians do not base the reliability of the Gospels on the determination of who wrote them, if sufficient evidence suggests that the traditional writers (Matthew, Mark, Luke and John) were the actual writers, then a *prima facie* (i.e., "on its face" or "without needing anything further") case is made that the Gospels contain the writers' own eyewitness accounts (Matthew and John), and the recording of others' eyewitness accounts (Mark and Luke). Evidence for or against authorship includes whether there are any historical references or traditions that attribute the Gospels to anyone other than the traditional writers.

*3. Were the Gospel writers honest?*

A key criterion for determining whether writers of ancient biographies were biased to the point of being unreliable is whether their accounts include embarrassing details. The inclusion of such details is strong evidence of historicity, in contrast to biographies that tell sanitized versions of a person's life. If the evidence shows the Gospels include embarrassing material, that is a valid argument that the writers were honest and objective and thus, we may infer, reliable.

*4. Are the Gospels the only reputable accounts of the life and teachings of Jesus?*

The four canonical Gospels (i.e., "accepted as Scripture by the Church," another way of saying "Matthew, Mark, Luke, and John") have come under fire indirectly by some who assert that the Early Church knew about certain "lost gospels" but deliberately excluded them from the New Testament. The question of "lost gospels" can be resolved by such factors as when they were written, who wrote them, and whether they add any reliable new material on the ministry of Jesus. If the evidence shows that the "lost gospels" were written much later than the canonical Gospels, by unknown writers pretending to be people mentioned in the New Testament, giving accounts and teaching the canonical Gospels contradict, then they can reasonably be excluded as being authentic accounts of the life and ministry of the historical Jesus.

*5. Can the original wording of the Gospels be established with a high degree of confidence?*

If the evidence establishes that the canonical Gospels are essentially eyewitness and primary source accounts, written by honest chroniclers of the life and teachings of Jesus, the question remains whether our existing copies accurately reflect the original writings (which are missing). The reliability of the Gospels depends on the quality of existing manuscripts (i.e., "handwritten copies"). If the evidence suggests that the original text of the Gospels can reasonably be determined with confidence, we can put to rest the often-heard argument, "the Gospels have been changed over the years."

If the evidence for the text of the Gospels is greater than the evidence for the text of other ancient writings that are never challenged on textual grounds, then a skeptic must choose either to agree with experts that the Gospel text is reliable or else to disregard all ancient writings because they are textually inferior to the Gospels.

6. *Do history and archaeology support the accuracy of the Gospel accounts?*

Some skeptics attempt to hold the Gospels to a higher standard than any other writings of antiquity, taking a "guilty until proven innocent" approach. If later evidence is found to substantiate certain Gospel accounts that were previously challenged, it would seem fair to give the "benefit of the doubt" to Gospel accounts that remain unconfirmed by history or archaeology. Additionally, if experts in the field of history conclude that the Gospels are generally reliable, then the burden of proof shifts to those who dispute Gospel reliability to provide equal or greater contrary evidence.

## A CUMULATIVE CASE

The case for the reliability of the Gospels is cumulative. If any of the six questions is answered with sufficient evidence to support the reliability of the Gospels, then an overall case for reliability increases. Some of the questions may carry more weight than others. For example, evidence that supports the reliability of the text of the Gospels does not mean the accounts they contain are true, any more than establishing the reliability of the text of Aesop's Fables makes them true. But establishing the textual reliability of the Gospels removes one possible objection to their reliability.

The stronger the evidence that supports answering the six questions in the affirmative, the stronger the case for the Gospels' reliability. The case for the Gospels is not undermined, however, because any single question lacks sufficient evidence to be answered in the affirmative. For example, the Gospels can still be considered reliable if written 100 years after Jesus, even though this would raise serious questions regarding the sources of their information. The Gospels can still be found reliable if their writers are anonymous, even though the questions remain regarding where the writers obtained their information. Similarly, the Gospels can still be reliable even if they show evidence of bias, since many historical writings generally considered reliable offer a rose-colored look at the people and events they cover. The Gospels can still be held reliable if other ancient writings are found that offer reliable new information about the life and teachings of Jesus. The Gospels can still be considered reliable if questions remain about the reliability of existing manuscripts. Finally, the Gospels can still be reliable even if some historians find certain references in the Gospels erroneous, since many of these same historians do not conclude that such discrepancies defeat general reliability, and since most ancient biographies contain discrepancies. Most important, if the evidence supports the reliability of the Gospels in all six areas under discussion, it would be reasonable to conclude that the Gospels are in fact reliable.

## CONCLUSION—IF THE GOSPELS ARE TRUE...

If the Gospels accounts are true, then we ought to consider them as a source of the very words of life that reveal the plan and acts of the Creator. This is the essence of why it matters as to whether the Gospels are historically reliable. If the Gospels tell the truth, then people can have confidence to accept that claim that there is a God who made promises to His creation, and intervened in history to fulfill those promises. Reliable Gospels mean thinking people have a rational basis for believing those promises. If the Gospels are true, then the "ultimate issues" for humanity, namely the questions of "why is there something rather than nothing?"[4] and "if someone dies, will they live again?"[5] are answered. If the Gospels do not tell the truth, then more than 2,000,000,000 people on earth who embrace Christianity should look for another path, because in such a case, Christianity would not provide intelligent answers to the ultimate issues. The stakes could thus not be higher. Either there is a God who has spoken and revealed

Himself through Jesus, or there is not. If the Gospel accounts are true, then there are compelling reasons to believe there is a purpose for our lives, and that eternity in Heaven is available to all who believe. Let's begin the investigation.

# CHAPTER ONE
# When Were the Gospels Written?

"But the Helper, the Holy Spirit, whom the Father will send in My name, He will teach you all things, and bring to your remembrance all that I said to you." John 14:26

**Issue:** Were the Gospels written when eyewitnesses to the life of Jesus were still alive, and do they contain material that would have been easily remembered?

**Argument:** The Gospels were written when eyewitnesses were alive, and they record the type of events that are easily remembered; they were written much closer in time to the recorded events than most other ancient biographies that experts consider reliable.

## EVIDENCE IN SUPPORT OF ARGUMENT

1. All four Gospels were written within the lifetimes of both eyewitnesses and hostile witnesses to the life and teachings of Jesus.

2. Several lines of evidence support the position that all four Gospels were written before A.D. 70.

3. Many of the events recorded in the Gospels are the type that are easily remembered, even decades later, because of the unique nature of the events and their highly emotional components.

4. Matthew, Mark and Luke may have used existing written sources as templates for their accounts.

5. The Gospels were written much closer to the time of the events they describe than most other ancient biographies.

## THE CONNECTION BETWEEN THE GOSPELS' RELIABILITY AND THE TIME THEY WERE WRITTEN

The first argument for the historical reliability of the Gospels is that the documents were written at a time when eyewitnesses were still alive and close enough in time that the events in the life of Jesus and His teachings could be accurately remembered and recorded. If the evidence suggests that the Gospels consist of early and eyewitness evidence for the life and teachings of Jesus, a strong presumption of historical reliability attaches to the writings.

## FICTIONAL ILLUSTRATION OF THE CONNECTION BETWEEN WHEN A DOCUMENT WAS WRITTEN AND ITS HISTORICAL RELIABILITY

### #1: THE ANONYMOUS DOCUMENT

Suppose a document was recently discovered during an excavation near the Coliseum in Rome. Scholars identified the document, written in ancient Latin, as a papyrus manuscript written around the year A.D. 200 containing unique accounts about Tiberius, Roman Emperor from A.D. 14-37. The manuscript does not indicate who the writer was, and no other sources survive that refer to the manuscript. The accounts in the document include details about Tiberius' habit of shouting *"vini vidi vici"* ("I came, I saw, I conquered") each evening from his palace balcony as the sun was going down. The manuscript makes other unique representations about Tiberius, but there is no corroboration from any ancient sources for any of the accounts, and there is no mention within the document as to how the writer obtained the information about Tiberius.

### #2: THE MARIO DOCUMENT

Suppose a document was recently discovered during an excavation near the Coliseum in Rome. Scholars identified the document, in ancient Latin, as a papyrus manuscript copied around the year A.D. 200 from an earlier original. Early 2nd century tradition identifies the original writer as Mario, who worked in the palace of Tiberius, Roman Emperor from A.D. 14-37. The document contains eyewitness accounts concerning Tiberius, and refers to "Emperor Vespasian, who recently seized power." The text of the document does not identify who originally wrote it, but the writer claims to have been the chief clothing purchaser for Emperor Tiberius. The document includes a unique reference to Tiberius' habit of wearing red flannel pajamas at night. The writer mentions several other personal habits of Tiberius, most of which are corroborated in other ancient sources. Three reliable early-2nd century Roman historians mention a man named Mario, and confirm that he was a confidant of Emperor Tiberius who also chronicled the Emperor's habits. The historians also mention that Mario was the chief clothing purchaser for Tiberius and lived in Rome until his death in the year A.D. 80.

### HOW CONFIDENT CAN WE BE ABOUT THE TWO ACCOUNTS?

Both the foregoing documents have data regarding Emperor Tiberius. It is possible that all the statements and claims contained in them are true. Virtually anything is possible in a contingent universe, however (except, perhaps, squeezing toothpaste back into the tube). We should care little for what is possible, and, instead, deal with what is plausible, what is probable, and what rises to the level of adequate historical certainty (about as good as one can get regarding ancient history). When we compare the two fictional accounts, it is clear which one should be given the strongest presumption of reliability. Here are the facts that render Mario's account historically probable:

### MARIO'S ACCOUNT:

1. The document purports to be written by an eyewitness to the life and habits of Tiberius.
2. Internal evidence supports the conclusion that the document was written at a time when eyewitnesses to the accounts were still alive (e.g., "Emperor Vespasian, who recently seized power" means the document was written shortly after Vespasian became Emperor, which historians agree took place in the year A.D. 69).
3. Mario, who died in A.D. 80 according to reliable sources, was alive when the document was likely written, confirming that Mario could have been the writer.

4. The document relays unique facts about Tiberius that only an eyewitness to the events would know.

5. The document's writer claims to be positioned to have first-hand knowledge of the unique facts presented.

6. The conclusion that Mario was positioned to know the details about Tiberius set forth in the document is attested by multiple, reliable early (i.e., within 50 years of Mario's death) sources.

7. The conclusion that Mario was the original author of the document is attested by multiple, reliable early sources.

8. Later tradition affirms that Mario was the writer of the document.

9. No tradition identifies anyone other than Mario as the author of the document.

10. Reliable early sources confirm the accuracy of many details within the document.

In short, according to both internal evidence (i.e., claims within the document) and external evidence (i.e., early sources and later tradition) Mario was in the right place at the right time to know about and accurately chronicle the habits of Emperor Tiberius. Considering all the evidence, is it reasonable to believe Mario's account regarding Tiberius' wearing red flannel pajamas, even though no known source corroborates the account? Given the known facts, it is quite reasonable. Mario's representations have earned the "benefit of the doubt," that is, a strong presumption that his account is true. Here are the facts that render the Anonymous Account less historically probable than Mario's account:

## ANONYMOUS ACCOUNT:

1. Written long after Tiberius, rules out the writer as an eyewitness or interviewer of eyewitnesses.

2. No corroboration by any other historical data or tradition.

3. No way to determine the sources of the accounts, whether written or oral tradition.

4. No way to determine whether the accounts are embellished or even fabricated.

5. Without the identity of the sources of the accounts, and without corroboration from outside historical sources, there is no way to confirm whether the accounts are accurate.

In short, the Anonymous Account *might* be entirely true, or contain kernels of truth, but there is no reasonable basis for confidence in the reliability of the accounts. Hence, no strong presumption of reliability attaches to the Anonymous Account.

## EVALUATING THE GENERAL RELIABILITY OF ANCIENT WRITINGS

When it comes to evaluating the general reliability of historical writings, we can employ many criteria to determine reliability. "General reliability" does not mean that every detail of every account must be perfectly accurate. Sometimes historical writings give condensed versions of events, provide approximations in numbers, paraphrase spoken words, write from a limited perspective that leaves out important details, misremember events, and pass along information from other sources that are erroneous.

The general reliability of historical writings should not be dismissed even when peripheral details are shown to be erroneous. As scholar Murray Harris notes, even "the presence of discrepancies in circumstantial detail is no proof that the central fact is unhistorical."[1] "General reliability" means there are reasons to accept the content as being true. These reasons include the writer's being at the right place, at the right time, or relying on sources that were in the right place, at the right time, so that the reader would expect the accounts to be accurate.

Most of these criteria for general reliability are rooted in common sense. For example, early evidence (i.e., closer to the events) is strongly preferred above later contributions.[2] In addition to early evidence, one of the strongest possible evidences is when early sources come from eyewitnesses who actually participated in some of the events,[3] what one historian refers to as "the rule of immediacy" and "the best relevant evidence."[4] Although historical writings can be reliable even when written well after the fact and by someone whose sources are not derived from eyewitnesses, a presumption of reliability is much greater when early evidence comes from participants in the events.

The above fictional accounts demonstrate the superior quality of early testimony, eyewitness testimony and corroboration from reliable sources. The application to the question of the reliability of the Gospels is apparent. If the Gospels contain early testimony that is connected to eyewitnesses and corroborated by reliable sources, a *prima facie* ("on the face of it") case[5] is made for their historicity. It follows logically that the Gospels are thus entitled to a strong presumption of accuracy, with a high level of confidence that the accounts are reliable. Once the presumption of accuracy attaches due to the breadth of quality testimony, the burden of proof[6] shifts to those who doubt the Gospels' reliability. The skeptic must, then, rebut the presumption of accuracy with competent evidence to the contrary.

## CALCULATING A DOCUMENT'S EARLIEST POSSIBLE DATE OF WRITING

Determining when an ancient document was written can be a challenge, since most ancient writings, including the Gospels, do not contain the dates they were written.[7] The approximate date an undated document was written is established by internal evidence, such as references within the writing to people, places and events, and external evidence, such as later authors' references to the writing in question.

One way to illustrate how to determine the *earliest* date for a writing is to examine the Book of Acts' two references to Roman Emperor Claudius.[8] The accepted dates for Claudius' reign are A.D. 41-54, meaning Acts could not have been written *before* the year A.D. 41. Acts 18:2 states that after Paul the Apostle arrived in Corinth, Aquila and Priscilla had "recently come from Italy" because "Claudius had commanded all the Jews to leave Rome." The banishment of the Jews from Rome likely occurred in A.D. 49[9]. If so, the events recounted through Acts chapter 18 likely occurred *shortly after* A.D. 49. Based on this, the *earliest* Acts could have been written[10] would be after A.D. 49. The Book of Acts ends with Paul in Rome, which most scholars agree was around A.D. 62.[11] Therefore, the *earliest* that Acts could have been completed is approximately A.D. 62.

## CALCULATING A DOCUMENT'S LATEST POSSIBLE DATE OF WRITING

Perhaps more important than calculating the earliest possible date of a writing is determining the *latest* possible date.[12] Once the latest possible date is reasonably established, the result is the probable range in which the writing occurred, namely somewhere between the earliest and latest likely dates.[13] To illustrate how this works, consider the issue of the date of John's Gospel. Internal evidence suggests a date *after*

A.D. 64, the commonly accepted date for Peter's martyrdom, since John 21:18-19 is commonly understood as a reference to Peter's death. External evidence supports the position that the Fourth Gospel was written *before* A.D. 125 (see discussion below of P[52], a fragment of John's Gospel dated around A.D. 125), and even before A.D. 100 (see discussion in Chapter Four regarding several lines of evidence that support the conclusion of a pre-A.D. 100 date[14]).

Internal evidence for the date of John's Gospel includes a reference within John (see discussion below on John 5:2) that supports a date of writing *before* A.D. 70, the apparent claim that the writer of the Gospel was an eyewitness to the events (John 21:24), and the absence of any reference in John's Gospel to the destruction of Jerusalem and the temple in A.D. 70. The argument about the destruction of Jerusalem is that anyone writing *after* A.D. 70 about Jesus and His disciples would surely have mentioned this seminal event,[15] in the same way that anyone writing about lower Manhattan in New York City after September 11, 2001 would reference the terrorist attack that brought down the twin towers of the World Trade Center.

As we see from the foregoing, various internal and external factors must be weighed to arrive at the latest possible date of a writing. Scholars looking at the same factors may still come to different conclusions about the latest date a work was written, so those seeking answers must determine which conclusion the evidence supports best. In the case of John's Gospel, it was almost certainly written after A.D. 64 and before A.D. 100.

## HOW IMPORTANT ARE THE DATES THE GOSPELS WERE WRITTEN?

Simply put, the more time that passes after an event or a person's life before a written record is made, the greater the chance for distortion. Thus, it is important to determine the approximate dates the Gospels were written to see if they were written close enough to the events to reduce the suspicion that the accounts were not accurately recorded. Several factors contribute to inaccuracies in historical writings, and these can even affect eyewitness accounts. For writings by eyewitnesses or based on eyewitness accounts, it is not uncommon for memories to fail, especially when a considerable time has passed between the event and its recording. Over time faulty recollections can be amplified, and even new memories created.

Finally, oral transmission (telling stories before they are written down) can add layers of tradition to actual events. For biographies made after eyewitnesses are gone, there is the risk that the writer used unreliable sources, including embellished oral tradition or written sources containing scribal alterations (changes made by those tasked with copying the written account). Although biographies written a century or more after a subject's life may still be keenly accurate, there is an increasing likelihood of distortion as more time has passed between a subject's life and the written account.

In cases where the writer is not an eyewitness, we must examine the sources the writer used, because under this scenario a biography is no better than the sources used to compile it. How does one know if the sources a biographer used are reliable? If the sources made errors, the biographer will certainly repeat those errors unless there is some way to know about the error and avoid perpetuating it. If a writer's sources are not known, there is no way to determine whether the writer used reliable sources. Although even biographies based on eyewitness accounts can have distortions, doubts about reliability are significantly reduced when a biography is demonstrably based on eyewitness accounts. Thus, if the Gospels were written relatively close in time to the life of Jesus, the presumption of accuracy is much greater than if the Gospels were written much later.

## WERE THE GOSPELS WRITTEN WHEN EYEWITNESSES WERE STILL ALIVE?

Given the universally accepted presumption that "earlier is better," the threshold question when investigating the issue of the Gospels as a reliable record of the life and teachings of Jesus is *when were the books written?* The answer has significant implications on the issue of whether the Gospels' content is accurately reported. If the evidence suggests the conclusion that the books were written at a time when eyewitnesses to the events were still alive, it is less likely that the Bible is merely a compilation of stories, passed down from one person to another over a long period of time before finally written down. Additionally, if the Gospels were written while eyewitnesses to the events were still alive, then hostile witnesses would most likely also be alive. If no contradictory testimony exists from hostile witnesses, more weight is added to the position that the biblical accounts are reliable.[1] Further, if evidence suggests the Gospels were written either by eyewitnesses or those who had access to the eyewitnesses, then the common allegation that the Gospels are the product of decades of oral tradition loses its appeal.

## ALLOWING EVIDENCE TO DETERMINE THE CONCLUSION

Regarding the Gospels, there are two competing views—skeptical and traditional. The *skeptical view* is that unknown writers wrote from a place far removed from the events many decades after the events. According to skeptics, today's Gospels are the latest form of stories that were passed along by word of mouth over many generations. As the stories were told and retold, the stories grew, to the point where it is now nearly impossible to separate history from legend.

The *traditional view* is the Gospels were written either by apostles or those closely connected to the apostles. If the writers used any written source as a template, that source would be even closer in time to the recorded events and teachings, and eyewitnesses would have been around to scrutinize the accuracy of any proto-Gospel source. Thus, historic Christianity holds that the Gospels are accurate primary source accounts of the life and teachings of Jesus.

How can one determine which view is true? If no one had biases, the evidence could be weighed in the way a juror is supposed to determine facts in a courtroom trial. The problem is, everyone has biases, whether they are conscious or unconscious. People's experiences often become obstacle to discovering the truth because they limit what is accepted before the evidence is considered. Similarly, past experiences can also induce people to accept certain claims uncritically. Both are extreme. Like a juror, those who want to know the truth about the Gospels should try to set aside prejudices and determine what is true based on the evidence. Does the evidence weigh in favor of the skeptical view or the historical Christian view? Is the most reasonable conclusion somewhere in between? Although the identity of the Gospel writers and the dates they were written are related issues, this chapter will address the question of the date of writing (Chapter Two will address the identity of the writers).

## MEMORIES?

Quick—name your third-grade teacher. Can't remember? I sure can't remember, although some of you may. For those who can remember, either you have a good memory, or something unusual must have happened in third grade that created a vivid memory.

The simple exercise about the third grade is relevant to the question of whether the four Gospels were written at a time close enough to the events for the writers to accurately remember and record the details. The question of whether the Gospels contain accurate recollections involves three important issues: (1) When were the Gospels written in relation to the events they describe? (2) Are the events the kind that would likely be remembered years or decades later? (3) Do the Gospels compare favorably with other ancient biographies in relation to the time gap between when the subject lived and when the biography was written?

## WHEN WERE THE NEW TESTAMENT BOOKS WRITTEN?

The date each Gospel was written is important, because books written 100 years after events could not be written by eyewitnesses, though it is possible that a book written 100 years after events could have been written by someone with access to eyewitnesses if the writer waited to write the accounts. Even though a written record of events made 100 years after the events may be accurate, the further removed in time a writer is from the events, the greater chance of distortion of the facts. Books written 10-60 years after events, however, have a greater chance of being written by primary sources, including eyewitnesses and those who interviewed and recorded the accounts of eyewitnesses.

Several factors help in determining when the Gospels were written, including the identity of the writers (see Chapter Two for a detailed discussion of the identity of the writers), whether any information within the writings helps establish the dates, and whether there are any sources outside of the writings that provide information regarding the dates of composition.

## QUESTIONABLE ASSUMPTIONS OF CRITICAL SCHOLARSHIP

Conservative scholars, meaning those who have a higher view of the historical reliability of Scripture, tend to conclude the Gospels were written earlier than their liberal counterparts. Sometimes disagreements on dates of writing are based solely on objective scholarship, where two scholars look at the same data and come to different conclusions. But often the differences are due to unwarranted assumptions or biases that cloud the scholar's judgment. For example, the 18th century liberal scholar Ferdinand Christian Baur, founder of the critical "Tübingen School" of the New Testament at Tübingen University in Germany, concluded that the Fourth Gospel, traditionally attributed to John the Apostle, was written around the year 170 by some unknown person.[16]

What was Baur's evidence for his conclusion? Actually, there was no direct evidence. His late dating for John's Gospel was essentially based on his theory that the Fourth Gospel shows a more developed theology than the *Synoptics* ("to view together," *Synoptics* refers to Matthew, Mark and Luke based on their similar approach in presenting the life of Jesus), and his assumption that no Jew living in the 1st century would have referred to Jesus as "God." Since John's Gospel makes numerous references to the divinity of Jesus, Baur concluded the Fourth Gospel must have been written much later, in the latter part of the 2nd century. Thus, his conclusion was colored by unproven (and later disproven) philosophical assumptions rather than by evidence.

Many people in Baur's time accepted his conclusions, kneeling at the altar of so-called "critical" scholarship, and in the process lost confidence in the Gospels as reliable sources for the life and teachings of Jesus. If Baur's theory was correct, then it was fair to ask how an unknown person who wrote 140 or more years after the time of Jesus could tell us anything we can trust about Jesus?

Baur's notion about the date of the Fourth Gospel was the forerunner of the liberal position that the Gospels contain "later Christological developments." This expression is a scholarly way of saying that Jesus was a mere Galilean preacher whose followers embellished stories about Him, and that the Early Church turned Jesus of Nazareth into the miracle-working Son of God and God incarnate.

## THE DISCOVERY OF EVIDENCE THAT DEFEATED BAUR'S THEORY

Unfortunately for Baur and those who drank at his well of *higher criticism*,[17] an early 20th century discovery sank Baur's theory that John's Gospel was written in A.D. 170. In 1934, some 75 years after

Baur's death, Colin H. Roberts identified a fragment of John's Gospel that scholars date around A.D. 125.[18] This small portion of John's Gospel (about the size of a business card), known as "P[52]," contains just a few verses from John chapter 18:31-33 and 18:37-38. It is the oldest confirmed manuscript (i.e., "handwritten copy") of the New Testament in existence.[19]

P[52] is one of the earliest examples of using a book form instead of a scroll. The book form of ancient writings, called a "codex," (plural, "codices") means the pages are bound together on one side just like modern books, whereas scrolls were pages bound together in a linear sequence and unrolled for reading.

After the discovery of P[52], the date for the writing of John's Gospel was pushed back from Baur's date of A.D. 170 to around the year 90. But even before the discovery of P[52] scholars such as Bishop J. B. Lightfoot[20] and even liberal theologian Adolph von Harnack[21] were voicing growing criticism of Baur. As a result, the Tübingen School was essentially abandoned. Recent scholarship confirms that the basis for the challenges to apostolic authorship of John's Gospel was mostly philosophical rather than evidential, and it is doubtful that Johannine (i.e., written by the Apostle John, Son of Zebedee) authorship has ever been refuted by coherent argument.[22]

Since the time of Baur, even some liberal scholars have been willing to re-think the dates of not just the Gospels but all the New Testament books. One prime example is John A. T. Robinson who wrote *Redating the New Testament*[23] (1976) in which he argues that the entire New Testament was likely written by A.D. 70. His main evidence is the total absence of any reference in the New Testament to the fall of Jerusalem in A.D. 70, the type of monumental event that would not likely be omitted if one were writing about events in Judea and Galilee after the year A.D. 70.

## CURRENT VIEWS ON THE DATES OF THE GOSPELS

Scholars currently propose the Gospels were written between the following years:

| | |
|---|---|
| Mark | 40-75 |
| Matthew | 55-80 |
| Luke | 55-85 |
| John | 65-95 |

SCROLL

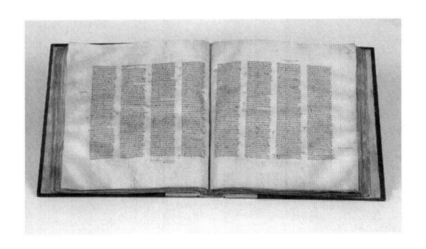

CODEX

## EVIDENCE FOR THE DATE EACH GOSPEL WAS WRITTEN

### MATTHEW

Most New Testament scholars today conclude that Mark was written before Matthew ("priority of Mark" theory), and that Matthew relied on Mark in many places as a template for order of events, inclusion of details and even wording. Some scholars, however, are not convinced and hold, along with Early Church father Augustine, Bishop of Hippo (ca 400) that Matthew was the first Gospel written.[24]

Most scholars today favor a date of A.D. 80 or later for the writing of Matthew's Gospel.[25] However, there is evidence that Matthew's Gospel, or at least some of it, was written around A.D. 62. Irenaeus (ca 180) was the Bishop of Lugdunum, what is now Lyon, France. According to church historian Eusebius (ca 350), Irenaeus stated, "Matthew published also a book of the Gospel...while Peter and Paul were preaching the gospel in Rome and found the Church."[26] Since Peter and Paul were in Rome together in the early 60s, Irenaeus' statement is evidence for an early date for Matthew.

Papias (ca 110) was Bishop of Hieropolis (modern Pamukkale, Turkey). Papias wrote five volumes, *Exposition of the Sayings of the Lord,* which exist today in only a few citations from Irenaeus and Eusebius. Eusebius reports that Papias claimed that Matthew wrote his *logia* ("oracles" or "sayings") in the Hebrew "dialect,"[27] which nearly everyone today agrees was Aramaic. No early copy of Matthew in Hebrew or Aramaic survives. Some have suggested that an Aramaic writing from Matthew's pen became the basis for a later, more expanded version of the life and teachings of Jesus, incorporating much of Mark's Gospel into the text. Though plausible, this explanation remains one of several possibilities. Here is a sampling of scholars who embrace an earlier date for Matthew than most:

- Daniel B. Wallace: 61-62.[28]
- R. T. France: the 60s.[29]
- Craig S. Keener: around A.D. 75.[30]

### MARK

Eusebius reports that Papias, writing about the year A.D. 110, stated that Mark wrote the recollections of Peter.[32] Clement of

Alexandria (ca 200), a Christian theologian and teacher of the pro-lific Christian apologist Origen (ca 184-253), adds that Mark's Gospel was written during Peter's lifetime,[33] although Irenaeus places it after Peter's death.[34] Early Church tradition relates that Peter was martyred by Emperor Nero around A.D. 65. Jerome, writing about the year 400, says Mark died in Egypt in the year A.D. 62,[35] meaning the latest Mark could have written his Gospel, if Jerome is correct, is A.D. 62. Not every New Testament scholar agrees with a date that early for Mark's Gospels, but the statement of Jerome, along with the traditions about Peter's death, would seem to shift the burden of proof to those who hold to a date later than A.D. 65 to come forward with sufficient evidence to overcome the evidence for an earlier date. Here is a survey from recent New Testament scholarship on when Mark's Gospel was written:

- James Crossley: late 30s to A.D. 45.[36]
- D.A. Carson and Donald Moo: the 50s.[37]
- R. T. France: no later than the early 60s.[38]
- Bart D. Ehrman: between 65-70.[39]
- Robert H. Stein: late 60s to 70.[40]

## LUKE

The Gospel of Luke is often referred to as "Luke-Acts," because the Gospel is part one of two parts based on the introductions in Luke 1:3-4 and Acts 1:1: "With this in mind, since I myself have carefully investigated everything from the beginning, I too decided to write an orderly account for you, most excellent Theophilus, so that you may know the certainty of the things you have been taught" (Luke 1:3-4). "In my former book, Theophilus, I wrote about all that Jesus began to do and to teach" (Acts 1:1).

Many scholars determine the date Luke was written from the likely date that Acts was written. The events in Acts end with the Apostle Paul's arriving in Rome to answer charges, a date commonly held to be around A.D. 62.[41] The last chapters of Acts reveal Luke's attention to detail, evidence that the events were still fresh in the writer's mind at the time they were written. Thus, a date close to the year 62 for the writing of Acts is warranted.

The lack of any reference to significant events that occurred from the years A.D. 65-70, such as the martyrdom of Peter and Paul, and the destruction of Jerusalem in the A.D. 70, is further evidence that Acts was written prior to the mid-60s. Since the Gospel of Luke is "part one" of Luke-Acts, Luke was written prior to Acts, likely A.D. 62 or earlier.

Despite the foregoing reasons for an early 60s date for Luke, many scholars conclude Luke's Gospel was written between 75-85[42]. The later date position is based on several factors, such as (1) Luke's version of Jesus predicting the destruction of the temple (Luke 21:20), which is more developed and thus believed to be written after the fall of Jerusalem (*vaticinium ex eventu,* "prophecy from the event"); and (2) Luke's usage of Mark, which requires a date for Luke long enough after Mark wrote for Luke to have access to it. Of course, if Mark is dated in the early 60s, then there was sufficient time for Luke to depend on Mark and still write before the Jewish wars began in the year A.D. 66 that led to the destruction of Jerusalem and the temple. A sampling of scholars' dating of Luke's Gospel is as follows:

- Carson and Moo: the 60s.[43]
- Darrell Bock: the 60s.[44]
- W. G. Kümmell: 75-85.[45]

## JOHN

Much debate surrounds when the Gospel of John was written, with dates ranging from A.D. 55 to A.D. 100. Church father Irenaeus (ca 200) and church historian Eusebius (ca 350) state that the Gospel of John was the last of the four Gospels written. If that is the case, the date of John's Gospel is still dependent on one's conclusion as to when the Synoptics were written. Thus, for those who conclude the Synoptics were written before A.D. 65, there is the possibility that John was written around 65 or shortly thereafter. For those who hold to a later date for the Synoptics, the writing of John's Gospel is necessarily pushed to near the end of the 1st century.

Recall the conclusion of liberal scholar John A. T. Robinson that the entire New Testament was written before A.D. 70. Robinson gives great weight to the fact that John's Gospel does not mention the fall of Jerusalem and the destruction of the temple that occurred in A.D. 70. Although scholars give no identifiable support to Robinson assigning a date of the

40s to John's Gospel, many scholars embrace Robinson's point about the glaring omission of any reference in John to the fall of Jerusalem. The omission is considered competent evidence that John wrote prior to 70, since there is no convincing reason for John to omit any reference to the fall of Jerusalem if, in fact, the destruction had already occurred. Those holding to a date in the 90s would counter with the point that enough time may have had passed (i.e., 20-30 years) so that the destruction of Jerusalem was no longer a major topic of discussion.

Competent internal evidence within John's Gospel also supports a pre-A.D. 70 date for John, namely John 5:2, "there is in Jerusalem a sheep gate...." This verse, with its verb ("is") in the present tense, describes a gate that did not exist after the A.D. 70, because the sheep gate was destroyed in A.D. 70 when Roman General Titus, son of Emperor Vespasian, leveled Jerusalem. Thus, if John's Gospel is describing the current situation as he writes the verse, it had to be written prior to A.D. 70.

Some commentators take John 5:2 as an "historical present," where the present tense is used to narrate past events. The Greek text of John's Gospel, however, does not support the "historical present" view, and it is more natural for the verse to refer to something existent at the time of writing.[46] Although the evidence for the date of John's Gospel is inconclusive, credible evidence suggests a date in the mid-60s, prior to the fall of Jerusalem. Here are scholars' conclusions regarding the date John was written:

- Wallace: A.D. 65 or 66.[47]
- Leon Morris: before A.D. 70.[48]
- Carson: between 80-85.[49]
- James D. G. Dunn: between 90-100.[50]

## THE BEARING OF THE GOSPELS' DATES OF WRITING ON THEIR HISTORICAL RELIABILITY

Scholars commonly accept that Jesus was crucified around the year A.D. 30, give or take 1-3 years. This means that the New Testament Gospels were written somewhere between 10 and 65 years after the crucifixion of Jesus. We need to put this "gap in time" between the events of Jesus' life and death and our biblical accounts into context.

To do this, we need to address several questions:

- Is the time gap short enough to support the reasonable likelihood that the events were accurately recalled and recorded by the Gospel writers?

- Were there any written accounts that about Jesus that pre-date the Gospels that the Gospel writers might have used as sources?

- Is there evidence that the writers' memories, and those of the witnesses they may have interviewed, were accurate?

Before addressing these questions, it is important to note at the outset that the consensus of scholars solves the question of whether the Gospels were likely written at a time when eyewitnesses were still alive with a clear "Yes."

## EYEWITNESSES ALIVE WHEN THE GOSPELS WERE WRITTEN

Previously, several lines of argument were raised that support a date for both the Synoptics and John's Gospel in the mid-60s or earlier. If true, this means the accounts were compiled no more than 35 years after the time of Jesus, and thus could clearly have been written while eyewitnesses were alive, and at a time when both friendly and hostile witnesses were also still alive. But what about assigning later dates to the Gospels, for instance, if Mark wrote some 45 years after Jesus, and John some 65 years after Jesus—do late dates necessarily defeat the reliability that is inferred from eyewitness accounts? No.

For example, let's say we accept the latest date ascribed by some scholars to John's Gospel, A.D. 90-100. If the writer was about 20 years old when Jesus was crucified, he and his surviving contemporaries would be around 80 years old at the time of writing. Though lifespans in the 1st century were, on average, much shorter than for people living today, many people did live to ripe old ages. Early Church writers indicate that John lived until nearly the year A.D 100 or even beyond,[51] which fact alone makes John a candidate for being the Gospel's author. Whether we conclude that John wrote the Fourth Gospel or not, the evidence supports the conclusion that John was alive when the Fourth Gospel was written.

We will address the challenge to John the Apostle's authorship in the next chapter, but suffice to say that even a late date fo John's Gospel does not rule out John as the author, nor of other eyewitnesses to the events having written (in the view of some scholars) or contributed to John's Gospel. And since the consensus is that the Synoptic Gospels pre-date John's Gospel, the evidence supports the conclusion that all the Gospels were written at a time when eyewitnesses to the events were still alive, regardless of whether early or late dates are assigned to the writing of the Gospels.

## ARE EVENTS DESCRIBED IN THE NEW TESTAMENT THE TYPE THAT ARE EASILY REMEMBERED?

### THE ROLE OF MEMORY IN RECALLING AND WRITING HISTORY

The study of memory is a fascinating area of inquiry. Most of us can relate to trying to memorize something, such as the periodic table of elements in a science course, the Presidents of the United States in a history course, or the state capitals in a geography course. What happens after being tested on the subject? We forget most of what we had memorized. This is an example of what is often called "short-term memory."

Short-term memory typically involves information that is not essential to our daily lives or survival, and is not highly unusual such as the name of someone you recently met, an address of a location such as a restaurant, a telephone number, or the exact date of an ordinary event in the past.

This type of information is sometimes stored for several seconds or up to a minute and then purged from our memories *unless* we rehearse it. Studies suggest that rehearsing information moves the items from short-term memory to long-term memory.[52] One of the reasons successful teachers repeat information is that hearers are more likely to retain it.

Long-term memory, on the other hand, involves the storage of information in our brains for many years, and sometimes our whole lives. Although neuroscience continues to explore how memory works, and what parts of the brain are involved in memory storage, there is general agreement that part of long-term memory is the ability to capture information such as specific events, called "episodic memory." Examples of episodic memories include weddings, meeting famous people, special performances (e.g., sports, music, speeches) and unusual events (e.g., planes flying into the World Trade Center towers).

For these types of events that exceed critical levels of surprise, researchers Brown and Kulik coined the expression "flashbulb memory," concluding that humans have a special biological memory mechanism that creates a permanent record of the details and circumstances surrounding the event.[53]

## REMEMBERING WITH ACCURACY

I often joke about having a photographic memory but being out of film. Seriously, I've been told that I have a heightened ability to recall data. Not that many events from my childhood are vivid, however, and most are long forgotten, although an occasional distant memory is triggered by a sight, sound or situation. Researchers try to determine why some events are remembered and others forgotten, and whether bad experiences are remembered longer than good ones. Research does suggest that older adults show a "positivity effect" in memory, remembering proportionally more positive events than younger adults.[54] Specifically, what kinds of events are most often remembered with accuracy? According to a 1977 study by Brown and Kulik, when a highly surprising event occurs, a special memory mechanism takes over, causing the moment to be recorded with picture-perfect accuracy.[55] Later studies confirm what Brown and Kulik found, namely that people vividly remember natural disasters, and even the time and place when they learned about shocking events such as an assassination or a terrorist attack.

## THE ROLE OF EMOTION IN THE ABILITY TO REMEMBER

One consistent element that enhances one's ability to remember is emotion. It is long known that experiences that elicit an emotional response are more likely to be remembered than those that do not.[56] Picture yourself in Judea, circa A.D. 28, as you observe Jesus speaking with Martha, whose brother Lazarus had died four days earlier. Martha heard that Jesus was coming, and went out to meet Him. After Martha told Jesus that her brother would still be alive if He had been there, Jesus tells her, "I am the resurrection and the life. He who believes in

Me shall live even if he dies." Martha's sister Mary then joined Jesus and her sister, and Mary also tells Jesus that if He had been there her brother would not have died. Seeing their emotion, Jesus wept, then proceeded to raise Lazarus from the dead (John 11:21-44). Would anyone who had been there and observed these events have forgotten them, even years or decades later?

Not likely.

Here is a simple list of questions that illustrates the point about memory. First, if you are married, do you remember the proposal? Also, if you have children, do you recall the birth of your firstborn? Next, if you were born before 1990, do you remember where you were when you first heard about the terrorist attacks against the World Trade Center and Pentagon on 9/11 (September 11, 2001)? Finally, if you were born before 1955, do you remember where you were when you first heard that President John F. Kennedy was assassinated? It is likely that if you are married, have at least one child, and are of sufficient age, you do remember the events, possibly even minute details, years, even decades later.

The Gospels contain many of the types of events that studies have shown are more often remembered with accuracy. These include Jesus' healing miracles, His statements that caused even His enemies to say, "No man ever spoke like this man" (John 7:46), His betrayal by one of His disciple, and His crucifixion, resurrection, and ascension into Heaven. Other "highly surprising events" include His feeding 5,000 with five loaves of bread and two fishes, walking on water and turning water into wine. These are the very types of experiences that memory experts tell us are not likely forgotten.

## REMEMBERING THE WORDS

A question related to the New Testament writers' accuracy in recording events is their accuracy in citing the words Jesus spoke. I have heard many moving sermons in my life, but I would be hard pressed to remember all the main points, much less repeat the sermons word for word. Regarding the Gospel accounts, there is some fluidity in describing events and reporting Jesus' words, as happens with virtually all historical accounts.[57] An example is Jesus' healing of the paralyzed man in a house in Capernaum along the Sea of Galilee, an event recorded in Matthew, Mark and Luke.

## FLUIDITY IN DESCRIBING EVENTS

In Mark's account of the paralyzed man (2:1-12) we read that four men carried a paralytic to Jesus, but could not get inside the house where Jesus was speaking. The men "removed the roof" and "dug[58] an opening," a reference to removing palm fronds and other thatched material that constituted a typical roof in Palestine in the 1st century. Luke's account (5:17-26) says the men carrying the paralytic "let him down through the tiles."[59] The reference to "tiles" on the roof would make more sense to readers outside of Palestine, because tiles were more common in other parts of the Roman Empire at the time.[60] Hence, parallel accounts within the Gospels sometimes include the use of dynamic equivalences when relating the story, a feature that suggests the writers, when appropriate, avoided wooden literalism that may have been an impediment to readers' understanding of an account.

## FLUIDITY IN RELAYING THE WORDS OF JESUS

In Matthew's version (9:2), Jesus says to the man, "Take heart, son, your sins are forgiven." Mark writes (2:5), "Son, your sins are forgiven." Luke's account of Jesus's words (5:20) reads, "Friend, your sins are forgiven." All three accounts agree on the main point--that Jesus forgave the man's sins. The variations in the salutation do not contradict the main point of conferring forgiveness.

## FLUIDITY IN DESCRIBING PEOPLE AND RELAYING THEIR WORDS

Similarly, Matthew relays that in response to Jesus' words, the "teachers of the law said to themselves 'This fellow blasphemes'" (9:3). Mark's version of the reaction of the teachers of the law reads that they were "sitting there, thinking to themselves, 'Why does this fellow talk like that? He is blaspheming! Who can forgive sins but God alone?'" (2:5). Luke's account adds that it was the "Pharisees and teachers of the law who had come from every village of Galilee and from Judea and Jerusalem" (5:17) and who were "thinking to themselves, 'who is this fellow who speaks blasphemy? Who can forgive sins but God alone?'" (5:21).

Matthew has the "bare bones" version. Mark adds that the teachers of the law were "sitting there." Luke adds more details, including mentioning "Pharisees" and the areas they and the "teachers of the law" had come from to hear Jesus. All the accounts contain the reaction of the religious leaders, namely that Jesus was blaspheming when He forgave the paralyzed man. This is the same way that eyewitnesses today describe an event, agreeing on the key elements but each emphasizing different details.

## ACCURATE DESCRIPTIONS USING DIFFERENT WORDING AND UNIQUE DETAILS

In the accounts of the paralytic in Matthew, Mark and Luke, Jesus points out to the religious leaders in the house that it is easier to say to the paralytic, "Your sins are forgiven" than "Get up and walk." Everyone in the room could observe whether a healing occurred, yet there was no visible way of confirming that the man's sins were forgiven. Jesus then proceeds to heal the paralyzed man, to everyone's amazement. The foregoing points are contained in Matthew, Mark and Luke, but the wording is different. This shows how historical events can be described accurately using different terms and including details that are not in other accounts.

If the Gospel accounts were commonly word-for-word the same,[61] the writers could be accused of collusion, since virtually no one remembers conversations and exchanges verbatim. Instead, the differences show earmarks of independent recollections. In a courtroom trial, if three people tell the exact same story using the exact same words, most observers would conclude the testimony was rehearsed, possibly to the point of calling into question their entire testimony. Slight variations on emphasis and detail, while describing the same main points as the others, however, adds credibility to the testimony as being independent and authentic. This helps explain why the accounts given by Matthew, Mark and Luke, despite relatively trivial variations, each contains the "authentic voice"[62] of the words of Jesus and others.

## WHEN ACCOUNTS ARE WORD FOR WORD

Several accounts in the Synoptic Gospels (Matthew, Mark, Luke) are word for word the same in two of the three or even in all three. Scholars have made various attempts to determine why this is so, and why, in other places, an event is described three different ways. A common solution to this "problem" is to postulate that Matthew, Mark and Luke may have used an existing written source as a template when writing their Gospels. In the case of Matthew and Luke, most scholars conclude that they used Mark's Gospel as a template, and perhaps some other, unknown source.[63] Luke tells us in his prologue (Luke 1:1-4) that he investigated everything "carefully" so that the reader might know the "exact truth."

If the Synoptic Gospel writers had a prior written account available, it may have been advantageous to use that account as a template. In this case the writers had the option of merely copying the words in the existing account, or of paraphrasing them. A prior written account may also have been used to refresh the Synoptic Gospel writers' recollections. This would be similar to the practice in a courtroom trial of showing a witness a document to refresh his or her recollection of events where the witness knows but cannot immediately recall precise details. Showing the witness a document or object can often jog his or her memory so that details can be elicited. The issue of whether and how the Synoptic Gospel writers used existing written sources in compiling their respective accounts remains a subject of debate, and is commonly called the "Synoptic Problem."

## HOW DO THE GOSPELS COMPARE WITH OTHER ANCIENT BIOGRAPHIES REGARDING THE GAP IN TIME FROM THE EVENTS AND THE RECORDING OF THE EVENTS?

Recall that the consensus of scholars is that the Gospels were written at some point between 10 to 65 years after Jesus' death. How does this time gap between the events and the recording of the events compare to other ancient biographies?

### COMPARING OTHER ANCIENT BIOGRAPHIES WITH THE GOSPELS

One of the leading figures of ancient history is Alexander the Great, who died approximately 325 B.C. His conquest of the known world by age 33 is a matter of study for students of ancient history. But what are the main sources for Alexander the Great, and do they always agree?

First, let's note that the primary sources written by people who knew Alexander or who gathered information from those who served with

Alexander are lost.[64] Today we rely almost exclusively on five later sources for the life of Alexander the Great, with the two best written by Arrian and Plutarch. The other three sources were written Diodorus of Sicily, Quintus Rufus and Justin.[65] Additionally, the five main sources sometimes disagree with each other on important details of Alexander's conquests.[66]

In the case of Arrian and Plutarch, there is no argument as to whether they were eyewitnesses or had access to eyewitnesses of the events of Alexander's life and conquests. Arrian wrote his history of Alexander, *Anabasis*, around the year A.D. 120, 450 years after the time of Alexander. Plutarch's *Life of Alexander* was written around the year A.D. 100, 430 years after Alexander's death. Historians consider these to be the best histories of Alexander that exist today. Of the three remaining biographies, the earliest is Diodorus (ca 45 BC), followed by Quintus Rufus (ca A.D. 50-75) and, finally, Justin (ca A.D. 140).

When the best sources on the life of Alexander the Great were written more than 400 years after Alexander's life, the gap of 10-65 years between the life of Jesus and the Gospel accounts of His life seems minimal. By way of comparison, if someone rejects the Gospels as a reliable source of information about Jesus based on how long after His life the accounts were written, then the biographies of virtually all ancient figures must similarly be rejected, since few, if any, were written as contemporaneously with the events as the Gospels.

For example, the Roman historian Suetonius (ca 120), wrote biographies of Julius Caesar, Octavian (aka Augustus Caesar) and others, in his *De Vita Caesarum* ("*Lives of the Caesars*"), which was written more than 150 years after Julius Caesar lived. The best sources for Roman Emperor Tiberius, who reigned at the time of Jesus' crucifixion, are Roman historian Cornelius Tacitus (ca 110) who wrote about 75 years after the time of Tiberius, Suetonius who wrote about 85 years after Tiberius, and Dio Cassius (ca 230) who wrote 195 years after Tiberius.

## CONCLUSION

Based on the accepted range of A.D. 40-95 for the writing of the Gospels, these books were all written at a time when eyewitnesses to the events were still alive. As F. F. Bruce says:

The evidence indicates the written sources of our Synoptic Gospels are no later than *c.* A.D. 60; some of them may even be traced back to notes taken of our Lord's teaching while His words were actually being uttered. The oral sources go back to the very beginning of Christian history. We are, in fact, practically all the way through in touch with the evidence of eyewitnesses.[67]

We will examine the evidence pertaining to whether the Gospels were written by the traditional authors Matthew, Mark, Luke and John in the next chapter. Here we note that the key events recorded in the Gospels are the type typically remembered with accuracy due to their highly emotional and extraordinary nature. When compared with ancient biographies of Alexander the Great and others, it is clear that the Gospels were written much nearer to the time of the events, at the *latest* 40-65 years after Jesus, whereas Alexander's best biographies are from over 400 years after he lived.

Unless critics can justify a special pleading that applies one set of criteria to the Gospels and another for all other ancient biographies, then the Gospel accounts must be approached as all other historical accounts and ancient biographies and thus appreciated as quite remarkable in the short gap between subject (Jesus) and biography (Gospels). The evidence supports the conclusion that the Gospels contain eyewitness and primary source testimony, written at a time reasonably close to the events, thereby defeating the challenge that they were written too long after the events to be considered reliable history.

# CHAPTER TWO
# Who Wrote the Gospels?

"This is the disciple who bears witness of these things, and wrote these things; and we know that his witness is true." John 21:24

**Issue:** Were the Gospel Writers Eyewitnesses or Interviewers of Eyewitnesses?

**Argument:** The Gospels were written by the traditional authors Matthew, Mark, Luke, and John.

## EVIDENCE IN SUPPORT OF ARGUMENT

1. The Gospels belong to the genre of ancient biographies.

2. The Gospels are not "anonymous" as the word is typically used.

3. No manuscripts of the Gospels or Church tradition ascribes their authorship of the Gospels to anyone other than Matthew, Mark, Luke, and John.

4. Matthew was an eyewitness to the life and teachings of Jesus, and several early writers confirm that he wrote the Gospel of Matthew.

5. Peter was an eyewitness to the life and teachings of Jesus, and Mark's Gospel consists of Peter's recollections, as told to Mark, whom several early writers confirm wrote the Gospel of Mark.

6. Luke was an investigative journalist who interviewed eyewitnesses to compile the Gospel of Luke, and several early writers confirm that Luke wrote the Gospel of Luke.

7. John, the Son of Zebedee, was an eyewitness to the life and teachings of Jesus, and several early writers confirm that the Apostle John wrote the Gospel of John.

8. In addition to the substantial evidence for the traditional authorship of the Gospels, most scholars do not consider the question of authorship of the Gospels crucial to regarding them as credible historical documents.

## WHAT TYPE OF LITERATURE ARE THE GOSPELS?

If a book starts out, "A long, long time ago in a galaxy far, far away," a reader should not expect the book to be an historical account. Literature prizes are awarded in various categories, such as fiction, biography and non-fiction based on the nature of the work. Though these categories, called *genres*, are often overlapping and imprecise, they are necessary to help the reader understand what the writer is attempting to communicate and what to expect. It would be difficult to fully appreciate literature if term papers were written in the same way as love letters, and if readers read them the same way.

With that in mind, what kind of literature are the Gospels?

• Do they attempt to accurately tell about the life and teachings of Jesus without any agenda coloring the accounts (objective history)?

• Do they tell embellished stories about an actual or mythological person named Jesus (historical fiction)?

• Do they tell a sanitized version of Jesus' life to convince the reader (misleading), and attack views contrary to those of the writer (polemic)?

• Do they tell accurately the story of Jesus (didactic) with a goal of convincing the reader (evangelistic)?

Within the Gospels we find a direct statement as to the intent of the writer. In the Gospel of John, chapter 20:30-31,[1] the writer acknowledges that the book contains selected accounts of Jesus' deeds and adds that the purpose of the writing is to bring the reader to the conclusion that Jesus is the Christ, the Son of God. The author's acknowledgment that he has an evangelistic motive for writing does not negate the Gospel of John's being objective history, even if the writer has an evangelistic motive for writing. On the contrary, the Gospel of John's writer appears to claim his account is that of an eyewitness and affirms his testimony is true.[2] The key issue is still whether the Gospel of John and the Synoptic Gospels intend to be reliable accounts, and are, *in fact*, reliable accounts.

Liberal 20th century Bible scholars such as Rudoph Bultmann argued that there was an "historical Jesus," but layers of oral tradition developed over time so that what the Gospels record is the "Christ of faith," not the Jesus of history. The Gospels were therefore not considered biographies, but traditions developed through the imaginations of early Christians. Attempts to arrive at the "historical Jesus" typically resulted in the conclusion that it was not possible to strip away the embellishments and myths to arrive at a true picture of Jesus.[3]

The paradigm shift in identifying the literary style of the Gospels came in 1992 with the publication of Anglican priest and biblical scholar Richard Burridge's book *What Are the Gospels? A Comparison with Graeco-Roman Biographies.*[4] Based on his analysis of the Gospels compared with ancient biographies of the same era, Burridge makes a compelling case that the Gospels belong to the genre of Graeco-Roman biography.[5] He concludes that the Gospels were ancient biographies of Jesus, in the same genre as Roman historian Suetonius' *The Twelve Caesars,* Plutarch's *Lives* or Tacitus' *Agricola.*

Since it is not disputed that ancient biographies have strong relationships with history, Burridge's identification of the Gospels as *ancient bioi*[6] was a death knell to the liberal notion that the Gospels were a type of religion fiction, divorced from history.[7] The view that the Gospels are ancient biographies is not new, however, since Justin Martyr (ca 160) referred to them as *memorabilia*[8] of the apostles, using a Greek word that was the same as the Latin designation used for Xenophon's biography of Socrates.

As a final word on the genre of the Gospels, it cannot be denied that the Gospels provide an historical context for the life and teachings of Jesus. Consider what the Gospel of Luke says (Luke 3:1):

> Now in the fifteenth year of the reign of Tiberius Caesar, when Pontius Pilate was governor of Judea, and Herod was tetrarch of Galilee, and his brother Philip was tetrarch of the region of Ituraea and Trachonitis, and Lysanias was tetrarch of Abilene....

This excerpt from Luke's Gospel is evidence of the author's desire to show that the events he writes about are rooted in history.

## EVIDENCE, WORLDVIEW, ASSUMPTIONS, PRESUPPOSITIONS

In order to conduct a proper historical investigation into the reliability of the Gospels, competent evidence (i.e., that which tends to prove the matter in dispute) must be adduced and weighed. Generally, evidence is either direct or circumstantial. *Direct evidence* is evidence that supports the truth of an assertion without the need to "connect the dots." *Circumstantial evidence* relies on an inference to connect it to a conclusion of fact. Thus, the weight of circumstantial evidence should not be discounted, and, contrary to a common assumption, people accused of murder are routinely convicted based on circumstantial evidence alone (i.e., no eyewitnesses). A famous case in point is the murder conviction of Timothy McVeigh, the man who carried out the bombing of the Murrah Building in Oklahoma City, Oklahoma on April 19, 1995.[9]

Another well-known story provides a vivid example of the difference between direct and circumstantial evidence: A man was accused of biting off the ear of another man during an altercation. A witness testified at a criminal trial that he was nearby the scene of the crime, had seen the altercation, and knew the accused was the perpetrator of the mayhem. When pressed by the defense attorney as to whether he truly saw the accused bite off the victim's ear, the witness admitted that he had not, but still believed that the accused had bit off the man's ear. The attorney did not know when to quit, so he pressed the witness, asking, "How can you be so sure that my client bit off the victim's ear when you admit you didn't see him do it?" The witness replied, "Because I saw him spit it out." Seeing a man bite off another's ear is direct evidence of what happened. Seeing a man spit out the ear is circumstantial evidence of what happened.

Direct evidence of historical events or sayings is hard to come by. Eyewitness testimony is rarely available, and when it is, it must be scrutinized to determine its reliability. In most questions about history, including the question of the authorship of the Gospels, circumstantial evidence is generally the determining factor for what is true. Unfortunately, presenting both direct and circumstantial evidence to determine the truth is not always successful, because people sometimes arrive at conclusions based on their worldview rather than the evidence. This is common among pseudo-skeptics as well as believers who accept truth claims uncritically.

An example of someone's worldview getting in the way of the facts occurred when the first settlers of the Australian continent discovered a creature that had a duckbill, webbed feet, and fur, and laid eggs but was a mammal. The Aussies shared the news of this strange creature with scientists in England, and even sent a pelt and a sketch of the animal. Although the pelt and sketch constituted direct evidence of the creature's actual existence, English scientists who saw the sketch and handled the pelt were dubious, thinking it was a joke because the characteristics of the animal we now identify as a platypus did not fit into their experience.

In short, since English scientists had never seen or heard of anything similar to what the Aussies presented, they assumed therefore it could not exist. It wasn't until the Australians shipped a live platypus to England for the scientists to examine that they finally changed their view. That which was once inconceivable to them became a reality only when they were confronted with physical evidence, despite already having direct evidence (i.e., the pelt and a sketch of the animal from Australia).

## ANTI-SUPERNATURAL WORLDVIEW

The influential Scottish philosopher David Hume did more than perhaps anyone to question the existence of miracles and thereby questioned the reliability of the Gospels that contain numerous accounts of miracles.

Hume's argument was essentially that in Jesus' time people attributed many things to gods, angels and demons, and were so philosophically unsophisticated and uncritical that they would believe in miracles without any evidence. Hume claimed that in his 18th century world no miracles were occurring as claimed in the Gospels, which he took as further support for his thesis that the miracles were products of fertile minds and theological embellishments. Hume considered miracles to be so highly improbable that he argued the miracle accounts in the Gospels should be rejected out of hand.

A contemporary of Hume, Bishop Richard Whately, responded to Hume with a clever essay on the existence of Napoleon. Whately made a case for the improbability that someone like Napoleon, who was not even French, could rally the flower of French youth, lead them to utter military defeat, then raise the French youth a second time, with the same devastating result. Whately concluded, in an essay entitled *Historical Doubts Relative to Napoleon Bonaparte*,[10] that the story of Napoleon was so improbable as to be unbelievable. Thus, Whately questioned whether Napoleon ever existed.

Whately's point was not missed by the readers of his day, since it was well known that at the time Whately wrote his essay Napoleon was living in exile on Elba. Many people today hold an anti-supernatural worldview, and therefore reject the existence of miracles on philosophical grounds rather than on evidential grounds. In response to the current anti-supernatural trend, in 2011 New Testament scholar Craig Keener published a two-volume compendium of over 1,000 miracle claims from the 20th and 21st centuries, with supporting documentation.[11]

In light of an increasing secularism in the Western world today, we must ask whether the reliability of the Gospels is questioned on evidential and historical grounds or on philosophical grounds. Historical inquiry is not aided by rejecting historical claims based on *a priori* assumptions rather than on the examination of evidence. Since it is difficult for all of us to lay aside our biases, the best we can hope for is an open mind and the willingness to follow the evidence wherever it leads.

## ANONYMOUS GOSPELS?

One of the criticisms leveled against the Gospels is that these primary sources for the life and teachings of Jesus are anonymous. Most Christians have never heard of this criticism and might respond by saying, "But it says in my Bible 'The Gospel According to Matthew, etc.'" The critic's point about anonymity is somewhat misleading. If someone says, "The Gospels are anonymous," the simple understanding of this claim is that we have no idea who wrote the Gospels, which of course is simply not true. Critics use the word "anonymous" to mean the names of the writers do not appear within the text of the Gospels,[12] i.e., "internally anonymous."

There are, however, solid clues within the text of the Gospels of Luke and John that support their traditional authorship. Regardless of how much weight is given to these clues, they create inferences that contribute to the circumstantial case for Luke and John being the authors. The inferences also counter the skeptical assertion that there is no way of knowing who wrote these Gospels. It would be more accurate for skeptics to say instead that they have "insufficient evidence" to conclude who wrote the Gospels.

The remainder of the "anonymous Gospels" criticism is essentially one from silence. Critics' contention that the original Gospel manuscripts did not contain the names of the writers is mere speculation because we do not possess the original manuscripts ("autographs") of the Gospels.[13] An unbiased assessment would acknowledge that there is no way to confirm whether the originals had the names of the writers or not, even though some conservative scholars concede that the titles of New Testament books were not part of the autographs, but were added later on the basis of tradition.[14]

Even if it is assumed that the Gospel authors' names were not part of the original writings (and there is no conclusive evidence for that assertion), many scholars conclude that the titles of the Gospels were added as early as A.D. 125.[15] Given the fact that our earliest copies that contain the beginnings of the Gospels of Matthew, Luke and John indicate they were written by Matthew, Luke and John, the skeptic's "anonymous" claim is not only misleading, but called into question by the earliest manuscript evidence.[16]

Regarding literary style, including vocabulary and grammar, critics contend that the disciples were not sufficiently sophisticated to write the Greek text of the Gospels. This, too, is a supposition that disregards evidence, such as Luke's being called a "beloved physician" (Colossians 4:14). The elegant Greek found in the prologue (1:1-4) of the Gospel of Luke is what we would expect from an educated author, such as a physician. The supposition that the Gospel writers were not sophisticated enough to write the Gospels further disregards the possibility that Matthew, Mark and John could have dictated their material to a scribe, called an "amanuensis," as the Apostle Paul did when he dictated the Epistle to the Romans to Tertius, who physically wrote the letter (see Romans 16:22).

As we will see later in this chapter, there are no surviving traditions identifying anyone other than the traditional writers as the source of the Gospels. Finally, critics need some plausible explanation as to how "anonymous" Gospels could have had such an impact on the Early Church if they were not attributed to someone trusted to know the facts.

## THE TELEPHONE GAME

In addition to the misleading assertion that the Gospels are anonymous, critics often add that the Gospels were likely written a long time after the events (which we addressed in Chapter One) at locations far removed from Palestine, by unknown writers who were not witnesses to the events, and who based their accounts on the "oral tradition" they heard. A less scholarly but common way of illustrating this criticism is to equate the origin of the Gospels to the "telephone game." Many have played the game where, in a room full of people, a phrase is whispered to a person, who whispers the phrase to the next person, and so forth, until it reaches the last person in the room. By the time the phrase reaches the last person, it is completely distorted from what it was originally. Thus, according to the critic, if the original stories of Jesus were transmitted by means of oral tradition before they were written down, what we have today is like the results of the "telephone game," namely an unreliable distortion of the actual life and teachings of Jesus.

If we assume that the original versions of the Gospels did not have the names of the writers at the beginning or somewhere in the text, how can we ever know who wrote the Gospels? Could they represent merely a collection of stories assembled by non-eyewitnesses, decades after the events, edited and redacted to create a fictionalized account of Jesus? Are the Gospels no more reliable than the result of the "telephone game?"

Although many critical scholars hold the view that the Gospels are anonymous compilations of later oral traditions about Jesus rather than reliable history, a careful examination of the evidence shows that such a radical view is unwarranted. There is considerable evidence supporting the Gospels' historical accuracy (see Chapter Six) and their authorship by the traditional writers as set forth below. In addition, the question of authorship is a separate consideration from historical reliability, i.e., anonymous documents can be reliable just as documents containing the author's name can be unreliable. Scholars who conclude the Gospels are anonymous still independently analyze the Gospels for historical accuracy and find many details corroborated by accepted facts from sources outside of the Bible.

## DISARMING THE "ANONYMOUS GOSPELS" INFERENCE

The identity of the Gospel writers is *not* essential for them to be considered as credible historical sources for the life and teachings of Jesus. Some people mistakenly believe that historical reliability of the Gospels stands or falls on the question of who the writers were, but this is not consistent with the views of current New Testament critics and historical Jesus scholars.

Experts can scrutinize the reliability of anonymous documents that present historical narratives using recognized criteria. These include comparing the historical references with known historical facts to see if they agree (see Chapter Six, below, regarding history and archaeology confirming Gospel and New Testament accounts), and by looking for earmarks of either honesty or bias on the part of the writers (see Chapter Three, dealing with the question of bias, and the "criterion of embarrassment" that gives weight to the honesty of the Gospel writers).

Thus, regardless of one's conclusion with respect to the traditional authorship of the Gospels, the reliability of the writings as accurate history remains a separate issue that scholars can independently investigate and address by adducing relevant evidence. Christian apologist William Lane Craig makes this point when answering a question about authorship of the Gospels by asking, "Who cares?" His provocative point is not that no one cares but that the question of authorship of the Gospels "is not crucial to regarding them as credible historical sources for the life of Jesus."[17]

Craig lists important factors for determining whether there is evidence that a particular saying or event is historical regardless of authorship and regardless of the general reliability of the document containing the saying or event.[18] But even if the identity of the Gospel writers is not "crucial," if the weight of the evidence favors the traditional authorship of Matthew, Mark, Luke, and John, a strong presumption of reliability should attach to both particular accounts and the general reliability of the Gospels. This is so because the traditional writers were either eyewitnesses who participated in the recorded events, or had access to the eyewitnesses, providing direct evidence in support of the accounts.

## EVIDENCE IN SUPPORT OF TRADITIONAL AUTHORSHIP OF THE GOSPELS

First, it was common in the ancient world for writers of histories and biographies not to include their own names. The most prominent ancient Roman historian, Cornelius Tacitus, is an example. Nowhere in his two major works—*Annals* and *Histories*—is he identified as the writer, yet no one disputes that Tacitus, writing in early 2nd century, was the one who penned these works. By way of comparison, the first direct attribution of any writing to Tacitus is from Tertullian, nearly 100 years after Tacitus wrote,[19] while attribution of the Gospels to their traditional authors began only a few decades after their commonly accepted dates of writing.[20]

Next, no evidence exists among early Christians that anyone questioned the authorship of the four Gospels. Although critics may deem this an "argument from silence," it highlights the fact that the "anonymous Gospels" allegation is of recent origin, based largely on assumptions of literary style. More important than evidence from silence, however, is the evidence from early Christian writers. Who did the generation of Christians after the apostles think wrote the Gospels? Since they were closest to the time the Gospels were written, their voices need to be heard.

### EVIDENCE FROM PAPIAS, JUSTIN MARTYR, IRENAEUS, TERTULLIAN AND EUSEBIUS

#### MATTHEW

Papias (A.D. 70-153) was the Bishop of Hieropolis in what is modern Turkey. He was a disciple ("hearer") of John and a companion of Polycarp[21] (A.D. 51-155). Writing during the reign of Emperor Trajan (A.D. 98-117) according to Eusebius, Papias discusses the authorship of the Gospel of Matthew and the Gospel of Mark. Regarding the Gospel of Matthew, Papias says, "Matthew recorded the sayings ("*logia*") in the Hebrew language...."[22] Irenaeus, Bishop of Lyons, wrote in his work *Against Heresies* (ca 180):

> Matthew published his gospel among the Hebrews in their own tongue, when Peter and Paul were preaching the gospel in Rome and founding the church there. After their departure, Mark, the disciple and interpreter of Peter, himself handed down to us in writing the substance of Peter's preaching.[23]

Papias' statement makes clear that Matthew wrote *something* regarding Jesus, and Irenaeus confirms that the *something* was a "gospel." There is no way to know positively whether Irenaeus was relying, in part, on Papias, or whether his information was independent of Papias. Since Irenaeus adds information that is not contained in Papias' statement about Matthew, Irenaeus must have had a source about Matthew's Gospel that was independent of Papias. The likelihood of an independent source helps defeat the theory that Papias was wrong about the authorship of Matthew's Gospel.

If the disciple Matthew was not the author of the Gospel that bears his name, there is no logical explanation why Matthew's name was chosen to give an anonymous Gospel legitimacy by appending apostolic authorship. Matthew would be an unlikely candidate for pseudo-authorship, given the fact that he does not figure prominently in any Gospel accounts and had been a tax collector, an occupation 1st century Jews considered loathsome. In addition to all the reasons why it would have been unlikely to fabricate Matthew as the writer of the First Gospel, no other person, apostle or otherwise, was ever identified as the writer of the Gospel of Matthew.

## MARK

Papias' writings were recorded by the 4th century church historian Eusebius as follows:

> The Elder used to say this also: Mark, having been the interpreter of Peter, wrote down accurately all that he mentioned, whether sayings or doings of Christ; not, however, in order. For he was neither a hearer nor a companion of the Lord; but afterwards, as I said, he accompanied Peter, who adapted his teachings as necessity required, not as though he were making a compilation of the sayings of the Lord. So then Mark made no mistake, writing down in this way some things as he mentioned them; for he paid attention to this one thing, not to omit anything that he had heard, nor to include any false statement among them.[24]

Thus, from Papias we learn that Mark, who may not have been an eyewitness to the events set forth in the Gospel of Mark, recorded the recollections of Simon Peter, who was an eyewitness to the events. During the 2nd century two other authors allude to the relationship between Peter and the Gospel of Mark: Justin Martyr (A.D. 100-165) and Clement of Alexandria (A.D. 150-215). Justin, around the year 135, writes, "It is said that he [Jesus] changed the name of one of the apostles to Peter; and it is written in his memoirs that he changed the names of others, two brothers, the sons of Zebedee...."[25] The nearest antecedent to "his memoirs" is "Peter," and the only text prior to Justin that refers to Jesus changing the names of James and John is the Gospel of Mark, further evidence for Papias' contention that Mark wrote Peter's accounts. These facts appear to refute the view of skeptic Bark Ehrman, who argues that Justin is referring to the Gospel of Peter rather than to a canonical Gospel.[26]

Some critics contend that Justin's reference to "the Gospels" ("for the apostles in the Memoirs composed by them, which are called Gospels,"[27]) is a scribal gloss in the margin of a manuscript that was interpolated into the text, and that Justin had no knowledge of the canonical Gospels.[28] The support for this theory is the weak assertion that since Justin only uses the plural "gospels" (Greek *euaggelia*) once in his writings, the sole reference must be an interpolation. This theory fails when we recognize that Justin makes 15 references to *Memoirs of the Apostles*, references that best fit the canonical Gospels. For example, Justin writes, "...in the Memoirs, which I say were composed by the apostles and their followers...."[29]

If Mark's Gospel was not written by Mark, there is no discernible reason for attributing it to Mark, or for that matter to anyone other than an apostle, since apostolic authorship conveyed authority per se, whereas non-apostolic authorship carried no such presumed authority. Early Church writers nowhere call the Gospel of Mark "Peter's Gospel," despite its universally recognized connection to Peter. The fact that there is also universal agreement among Early Church writers that Mark is the author of the Second Gospel is a further argument that early Christians were honest in reporting the facts.

## LUKE

Regarding the Gospel of Luke, Irenaeus wrote: "Luke, the follower of Paul, set down in a book the gospel preached by his teacher."[30] Most scholars date the earliest list of New Testament books, called the "Muratorian Canon," to around the year A.D. 170,[31] and it lists Luke as the author of the Gospel that bears his name. Although Luke's name does not appear within the text of the Gospel of Luke, the oldest existing copy of Luke, manuscript P[75], bears the title, "Gospel According to

Luke." P[75], part of a collection of Greek documents discovered in 1952, dates to around the year 200. Church Father Tertullian (ca 160-225) attributes the Gospel of Luke to Luke.[32]

If Luke did not write the Gospel that bears his name, it is difficult to conceive of a plausible reason for appending Luke's name. Luke was not an apostle, not likely an eyewitness to the events recorded in the Gospels, and was not connected to any of the Twelve. His sole credential was that he was a companion of Paul. Thus, if the Gospel attributed to Luke is truly anonymous as some skeptics claim, the burden is on the skeptic to provide a convincing reason why the ruse involved using Luke's name as the writer.

## JOHN

As to the Gospel of John, Irenaeus writes: "Then John, the disciple of the Lord, who also leaned on his breast, himself produced his Gospel, while he was living in Ephesus in Asia."[33] Irenaeus had been a student of Polycarp (A.D. 69-155), Bishop of Smyrna, and Polycarp had been a disciple of John the Apostle (confirmed by Tertullian, A.D. 155-240). Thus, Irenaeus heard accounts from Polycarp that came directly from people such as the Apostle John, who had personal contact with Jesus. With solid evidence supporting the Apostle John as the author of the Gospel that bears his name, it becomes clear that critics rely on philosophical as opposed to evidential grounds to challenge Johannine (i.e., written by John the Apostle) authorship, a point that Gospel scholar Andreas J. Köstenberger underscores.[34]

## DIRECT EVIDENCE FOR ALL FOUR GOSPELS COMBINED

### DIRECT EVIDENCE FROM TATIAN

Around the mid-2nd century Assyrian Christian apologist Tatian (ca 160-175) created the *Diatessaron* ("out of four"), the first "Gospel harmony," using exclusively the canonical Gospels in weaving together a single narrative. The *Diatessaron* is evidence that, by the mid-2nd century, the canonical Gospels, and they alone, were considered authoritative accounts of the life and teachings of Jesus.

## DIRECT EVIDENCE FROM THE MURATORIAN CANON

The Muratorian Canon lists four Gospels, although the names of the first two are missing because the manuscript lacks the beginning page. Luke and John are mentioned by name as the writers of the Third and Fourth Gospels.

## DIRECT EVIDENCE FROM GOSPEL MANUSCRIPTS

The earliest copies of each Gospel that contain the beginning portion all attribute them respectively to Matthew, Mark, Luke or John. In fact, no manuscripts of the Gospels that contain the beginning of any Gospels fail to attribute them to Matthew, Mark, Luke or John. In short, no Gospel manuscript is "anonymous," starting with the earliest, e.g., P[66] and P[75] (ca 200).[35]

## SUMMARY OF DIRECT EVIDENCE FOR AUTHORSHIP OF THE GOSPELS

### GENERAL

Justin Martyr (ca 135-150) references the "memoirs of the apostles" 15 times in two treatises and uses the terms "gospel" and "gospels."[36] Tatian (ca 160-175) uses the canonical Gospels exclusively in creating his Gospel harmony ("*Diatessaron*"). All Greek manuscripts of the Gospels that contain the beginning portion are attributed to Matthew, Mark, Luke or John, with none being "anonymous."

### MATTHEW

Papias (ca 98-117) ascribes sayings ("logia") of Jesus to Matthew, whom he said wrote "in the Hebrew language."

Irenaeus (ca 180) wrote that Matthew "published his gospel among the Hebrews in their own tongue."

### MARK

Papius (ca 98-117) wrote that Mark was the "interpreter of Peter" and wrote down "accurately" all that Peter mentioned. Papias further wrote that Mark "made no mistake," did not omit anything he had heard, and did not "include any false statement." Justin Martyr (ca 135) in writing about "Peter's memoirs," mentions an account that is recorded only in the Gospel of Mark, further attestation that Mark wrote the recollections of the Apostle Peter. Anti-Marcionite Prologue to Mark (ca 160-180) ascribes authorship of Mark's Gospel to Mark.

## LUKE

The Anti-Marcionite Prologue to Luke (ca 160-180) ascribes authorship of Luke's Gospel to Luke.

The Muratorian Canon (ca 170) lists Luke as the author of the Gospel of Luke.

Irenaeus (ca 180) wrote that "Luke, the follower of Paul, set down in a book the gospel...."

P[75] (ca 200), also known as "Bodmer Papyrus XIV," the oldest existing copy of Luke's Gospel, bears the title, "Gospel According to Luke."

Tertullian (160-225) ascribes the Gospel of Luke to Luke.

## JOHN

The Anti-Marcionite Prologue to John (ca 160-180) ascribes authorship of John's Gospel to John.

The Muratorian Canon (ca 170) names John as the author of the Fourth Gospel and assumes that the author of the Gospel of John is the same person who wrote the First Epistle of John and one other Epistle.

Irenaeus (ca 180), a disciple of Polycarp, who was a companion of Papias, and fellow "hearers of John" wrote that John "produced his Gospel...."

## CIRCUMSTANTIAL EVIDENCE FOR TRADITIONAL GOSPEL AUTHORSHIP

### EVIDENCE FROM THE "ANTI-MARCIONITE PROLOGUES"

"Prologues" ("introductions") to Mark, Luke and John exist in a few dozen Greek manuscripts that were identified by Dom Donatien De Bruyne as having been written shortly after the Marcionite crisis (ca 144), hence, the label "Anti-Marcionite Prologues." Marcion was excommunicated from the Church in Rome and labeled a heretic for his Gnostic views about God and his rejection of all Jewish elements in the New Testament. Marcion rejected the Gospels of Matthew, Mark and John, and accepted only the Gospel of Luke and Paul's letters as Scripture (the "Marcion canon"). De Bruyne concludes that the prologues show the tradition in the Early Church regarding the authorship of the Gospels, prompted by the unorthodox views of Marcion.[37] Liberal Lutheran scholar Adolph von Harnack agreed with De Bruyne's assessment regarding the dates, concluding the Prologues were written between A.D. 160-180.[38] Some scholars, however, give the Anti-Marcionite Prologues much later dates, e.g., 3rd or 4th century.[39]

### EVIDENCE FROM THE DIDACHE

The *Didache* ("Teaching *of the Twelve Apostles*") is a 1st century text (ca 90) that contains many references to Matthew, Mark and Luke ("Synoptic Gospels"). These include the Lord's Prayer found in Matthew and Luke, which is introduced in the *Didache* with the words, "...pray like this, just as the Lord commanded in His Gospel." The wording of the *Didache* is strikingly like the Synoptic Gospels.[40]D

### EVIDENCE FROM LETTERS OF IGNATIUS OF ANTIOCH

Around the year A.D. 105 Ignatius of Antioch wrote several letters[41] containing wording from the canonical Gospels.[42] Jerome (ca 390) considered Ignatius to be one of the Apostle John's disciples.[43] Ignatius was the second or third Bishop of Antioch, Syria, following the Apostle Peter. Roman authorities arrested him sometime around 105, and he wrote his letters en route to Rome where he was tried and eventually executed. His last letter was to Polycarp, Bishop of Smyrna, who tells of Ignatius' martyrdom in his *Letter to the Philippians* 9:1-2 (ca 120).

Ignatius' knowledge of the Gospel of John can be taken as proved,[44] and according to J. B. Lightfoot the whole passage of Ignatius' *Letter to the Romans* (7:2ff) "is inspired by the Fourth Gospel."[45]

### EVIDENCE FROM THE EPISTLE OF BARNABAS

Although scholars agree this letter was not written by the same Barnabas who was Paul's companion on the First Missionary Journey according to the Book Acts (13:1ff), it was likely written between A.D. 100-115. In *Barnabas* 4.14 there is a reference to Jesus' words found in the Synoptic Gospels, "many are called but few chosen." *Barnabas* introduces this phrase with the words, "It is written," the same term[46] used to introduce Old Testament passages. This is perhaps the earliest example outside of the New Testament of a Gospel being elevated to the same level of authority as Old Testament Scripture. Additionally, the *Epistle of Barnabas* contains other likely references to the Synoptic Gospels.

## EVIDENCE FROM THE MURATORIAN CANON (CA 180)

The Muratorian Fragment is missing the beginning and starts with, "...at which nevertheless he was present, and so he placed them (2) The third book of the Gospel is that according to Luke...the fourth of the Gospels is that of John, of the disciples." The references to "third" and "fourth of the Gospels" makes clear that the writer knows of four Gospels, and the fragmentary clause at the beginning appears to mean that Mark arranged the material of his Gospel as directed by Peter, who was present and participated in the events Mark narrates.

## INTERNAL EVIDENCE

In addition to the multiple, early references from Church Fathers that confirm the Gospel authors were Matthew, Mark, Luke and John, there is considerable internal evidence for traditional authorship. For example, the Gospel of Luke contains a prologue in which the writer presents himself as an investigative journalist. Luke 1:3-4 says the writer has "investigated everything carefully from the beginning" so that the reader "might know the exact truth" about the things he had been taught. The Book of Acts appears as "part two" of the Gospel of Luke, being dedicated to the same person, "Theophilus." Many scholars thus refer to "Luke-Acts" as one work divided into two parts (perhaps due to the length of the combined treatises, which together would have greatly exceeded the length of the average scroll of the time). Thus, there is strong evidence that Luke, the companion of Paul, wrote Acts, as "part two" of his original treatise of which the Gospel of Luke was "part one."

Since there is compelling evidence that Luke was the author of both the Gospel of Luke and the Book of Acts, the accuracy of factual statements in Acts supports the conclusion that Luke's Gospel is similarly accurate. Archaeologist Sir William Ramsay was taught the critical view that the Book of Acts was not written by Luke but instead by some unknown writer around A.D. 170 attempting to unite the Jewish followers of Jesus with the Hellenistic ("Greek") followers of Paul. Out of necessity Ramsay began using the Book of Acts for his research of Asia Minor. He discovered such accuracy in Acts that he concluded Luke must be the writer, for no one writing in the late 2nd century could have known the precise details recorded in Acts. Ramsay referred to Luke as "a historian of the first rank; not merely are his statements of fact trustworthy...this author should be placed along with the very greatest historians."[47] Classical scholar Colin J. Hemer concurs with Ramsay, documenting 84 facts in the last 16 chapters of Acts that history and archaeology have confirmed.[48]

Thus, since the evidence supports that the writer of Acts was Luke, and the Gospel of Luke is part one of "Luke-Acts," then it logically follows that Luke also wrote the Gospel that bears his name.

Internal evidence supporting the Apostle John's authorship of the Gospel of John includes the claim that it was written by an eyewitness to the crucifixion of Jesus: "And he who has seen has borne witness, and his witness is true; and he knows that he is telling the truth, so that you may believe" (John 19:35). There is considerably more internal evidence supporting Johannine authorship of the Gospel that bears John's name.[49]

## CONCLUSION

Eyewitness accounts and records of interviews with eyewitnesses are not affected by oral tradition and cannot be compared with the "telephone game." The external and internal evidence lead to the conclusion that the authors of the Gospels were indeed Matthew, Mark, Luke, and John. Based upon that conclusion, we have Matthew and John who were eyewitnesses, Mark, who wrote the recollections of eyewitness Peter, and Luke, who interviewed eyewitnesses.

Critical theories abound that question the Gospels' authorship, starting with the misleading statement that "the Gospels are anonymous." In fact, the Gospels are "anonymous" only in the same way that Roman historian Tacitus' writings are "anonymous." No one seriously doubts the authorship of Tacitus' two major works. Similarly, no one should deny that there is substantial evidence, both external and internal, direct and circumstantial, that supports the traditional authorship of the Gospels. Therefore, those who accept the Gospels as reliable eyewitness accounts of the life and teachings of Jesus do so based on a significant amount of competent evidence.

# CHAPTER THREE
## Honest or Biased?

**Issue:**    Do the Gospel writers show evidence of honesty in reporting the life and teachings of Jesus?

**Argument:**    The criterion of embarrassment is strong evidence that the Gospel writers were honest in their accounts of Jesus and the Disciples.

### EVIDENCE IN SUPPORT OF ARGUMENT

1. The fact that the Gospels writers were followers of Jesus does not disqualify them from honestly reporting the events as they occurred, and their accounts would be questionable if they remained neutral after witnessing the events recorded in the Gospels.

2. Bias is not implied merely because the Gospel writers had an evangelistic or theological reason for writing.

3. Evidence that the Gospel accounts are embellished is weak, at best, and is arguably nonexistent. Many historical writers who are considered reliable embellish certain facts.

4. A compelling reason to conclude that the Gospel writers were honest is the criterion of embarrassment, and the inclusion of unflattering accounts about Jesus and His disciples is strong evidence of authenticity.

5. The criterion of embarrassment is parallel to the legal notion of "declaration against interest" which makes otherwise inadmissible testimony admissible in court because of the strong likelihood the declaration is true.

6. The Gospels provide embarrassing details in numerous instances, such as the disciples falling asleep in the Garden of Gethsemane after Jesus told them to "watch and pray" and Peter's selfishly denying Jesus three times.

7. It is not reasonable to conclude the Gospel writers were dishonest in their accounts, because dishonesty violated the

teaching of Jesus, and the writers did not stand to gain from dishonesty but instead suffered persecution and death for their accounts.

## EVERYONE HAS BIASES, WHETHER WE ADMIT TO THEM OR NOT

Many years ago I was about to watch my older brother Don play a Pony League (13-14-year-olds) baseball game on a Saturday morning. Before the game started the gregarious announcer, Mr. Bohnett, informed the spectators they were short one umpire, and asked, "Is there an unbiased father in the stands who would be willing to umpire?" After a couple of minutes, when no one had come forward, Mr. Bohnett brought laughter when he asked, "Is there a *biased* father in the stands who would be willing to umpire?"

As a noun, the word *bias* is defined as "prejudice in favor of or against one thing, person, or group compared with another, usually in a way considered to be unfair." Synonyms of *bias* include *prejudice,*[1] *partiality, partisanship* and *favoritism.* The jury instructions that judges read to the juries in criminal cases in California includes the following regarding whether a witness is believable:

> The testimony of each witness must be judged by the same standard. You must set aside any bias or prejudice you may have, including any based on the witness's gender, race, religion, or national origin.[2]

The jury instruction does not tell jurors *how* to "set aside bias or prejudice," since often our biases are deeply ingrained in our subconscious. But one thing is clear from this instruction: bias and prejudice are bad when it comes to judging someone's testimony. This can be a two-edged sword, because a question often raised about the trustworthiness of the Gospel writers is, "How can I believe the testimony of the Gospel writers, since they were converts?" This question assumes the Gospel writers are to be looked at with a jaundiced eye because they were *believers,* and, therefore, *biased.*

The irony is that a person questioning the reliability of the Gospel writers because of their belief in Jesus reveals the person's bias by assuming conversion to Christianity disqualifies the writers as reliable witnesses! In fact, dismissing the testimony of the Gospels because of the writers' belief in Jesus violates the jury instruction about setting aside "bias or prejudice...including any based on the witness's...religion...."

## WHEN A WITNESS' BIAS IS RELEVANT

The previously mentioned jury instruction goes on to say: "In evaluating a witness' testimony, you may consider anything that reasonably tends to prove or disprove the truth or accuracy of that testimony." This is followed by a long list of factors the jurors *may* consider, including:

- How well was the witness able to remember and describe what happened?

- How well could the witness see, hear or perceive the things about which the witness testified?

- Was the witness's testimony influenced by a factor such as bias or prejudice, a personal relationship with someone involved in the case, or a personal interest in how the case is decided?

The first two factors, as applied to the reliability of the Gospels, are the very factors addressed previously in Chapters One (i.e., how well could the writers remember the events they wrote about?) and Two (who wrote the accounts, and does the evidence suggest they are firsthand accounts?). In this chapter we consider the third factor from the jury instructions—do the Gospel accounts show that the writers' testimony was influenced by bias? If so, *then* it would be reasonable to question the accuracy of the Gospel accounts. But does their content reveal the author bias, or, just the opposite, that the writers were honest and accurate?

## DETECTING BIAS

During my nearly 10 years as a radio talk show host, I became aware of how easy it is for my own personal biases to creep in to topics being discussed on my show. It was even easier to detect biases in others, especially in the way that people and organizations were described. For example, one of the colorful political figures of the 1980s and 1990s was Lyndon LaRouche, who ran for the Democrat Party nomination for President of the United States seven times from 1976 to 2004. When I interviewed LaRouche, I found him to be very intelligent and well-spoken, notwithstanding his known socialist agenda and out-of-the-mainstream views.

What I found interesting was how others described LaRouche, both in broadcast and print media. It was never merely "Lyndon LaRouche..." or "Presidential candidate Lyndon LaRouche." Instead, it was always, without exception, "political extremist Lyndon LaRouche." I remarked on more than one occasion that media had affixed "political extremist" to LaRouche to the point that it sounded like the appendage was part of his name.

What does the consistent use of "political extremist" say about those who used the terms? Bias. Journalists could not resist marching in lock step with others in the media, effectively marginalizing LaRouche by their description of him as a "political extremist."

Another example of how bias affects how we describe things became apparent when Operation Rescue came to Southern California. Operation Rescue was a pro-life movement that often utilized the tactic of blocking access to abortion clinics in efforts to save the unborn. Operation Rescue consisted of ordinary people who, from my experience of them, were mostly upstanding citizens in the community. Yet these folks subjected themselves to arrest for trying to prevent pregnant woman from having abortions and thus protecting unborn babies.

When Operation Rescue came to Southern California where I lived at the time, it created quite a controversy. An "all-news" Los Angeles radio station's reporting on the activities of Operation Rescue was quite revealing. Not being content with merely calling them "Operation Rescue," or even "anti-abortion Operation Rescue," the news station referred to the pro-life group as "militant, anti-choice Operation Rescue." I contacted the station and told them that their description of Operation Rescue was not "reporting the news" but was *advocacy*, because they had chosen adjectives to describe the group that revealed an inherent condemnation (i.e., *militant* and *anti-choice*). A purported news station had chosen sides, and it colored the station's efforts to present the facts. Bias had crept in.

## CONSCIOUS AND UNCONSCIOUS BIAS

Bias can be conscious or unconscious. Years ago on the Island of Martinique in the Caribbean, I took a taxi ride from the airport to the capital of Fort-de-France. On Martinique, as in several countries in the world, people drive cars on the left side of the road, unlike in America, where we drive on the right. A fellow passenger in my cab who was from the United States, asked the driver, "What's it like to drive on the *wrong* side of the road?" The cab driver slowly turned and said, "Is not the *wrong* side. Is the *left* side."

The passenger's question illustrated a bias, what is sometimes called the "egocentric predicament," where we see our own experiences as "right," and anything different as "wrong." This is an unconscious bias. There is also a conscious bias, where facts and truth are "shaded" to induce a reader or listener to arrive at the same conclusion the writer or speaker holds. How can someone know whether historical sources in general, or particularly the Gospels, contain either conscious or unconscious biases that affect the question of their reliability?

## A STATED GOAL
The traditional writers of the Gospels were followers of Jesus, but they did not start out as followers. Instead, they were convinced by what they saw and heard. Similarly, Jesus' brothers James and Jude, both writers of New Testament Epistles, were among Jesus' family who at one point worried that Jesus had lost His mind (Mark 3:21, "...his family...went to take charge of Him, for they said, 'He is out of His mind.'"). Yet they, too, eventually became followers of Jesus.

Being convinced of a fact, such as Jesus being the Messiah, is not "bias" or "prejudice." As we set forth in Chapters One and Two, evidence supports the conclusion that the Gospel writers either themselves witnessed, or interviewed others who witnessed Jesus uttering profound teachings, performing miracles, and showing Himself alive after He had been crucified. Thus, the writers' view of Jesus was based on experience and reason, not on bias or prejudice.

The Apostle John was certainly convinced based on his experience that Jesus was the divine Messiah. John does not hide the fact that he wants others to read about what he had seen and heard, then come to the same conclusion he had--that Jesus is the Christ. He clearly states that he has written his Gospel so that the reader "might believe that Jesus is the Christ, the Son of God, and that by believing you may have life in His name" (John 20:31).

Based on John's own words, his Gospel has an evangelistic purpose, that is, even though he was reporting events and speeches much like a typical ancient biographer would do, he is reporting so that people will be convinced, as he was, that Jesus is the only One who can save people from their sins. Thus, John is not biased or prejudiced toward Jesus because he was convinced based on his experience. There is no unfair "pre-judgment" (i.e., "prejudice") when one's testimony is based on what one heard and saw. And John does not conceal his hope that those who read his account would find what he found.

## EMBELLISHMENT OR EMBARRASSMENT?

Skeptics of Christianity often accuse the New Testament writers of embellishment and exaggeration. It is true that many writers throughout history have embellished their accounts. One of these writers is Flavius Josephus, the 1st century Jewish historian whose works include references to Jesus.[3] Josephus fought against the Romans until it was either "surrender or die." Though Josephus surrendered, he eventually became a chronicler of the Jewish Wars (A.D. 66-70) and also of Roman emperors.

Josephus embellishes Old Testament stories[4] as well as his involvement in the Jewish Wars that led to the destruction of Jerusalem in A.D. 70. Like Thucydides and Polybius, Josephus embellishes, distorts and invents for the purpose of enhancing the dramatic effect of his accounts.[5] Despite the embellishments, Josephus is considered generally reliable as an historian.

Is there evidence that the New Testament writers similarly embellished or exaggerated their accounts? Perhaps the best way to resolve the question is to go to the most scrutinized event in the New Testament—the resurrection of Jesus from the dead. Did the writers make up the resurrection appearances of Jesus? Assuming for the moment that they did, what was their purpose? It makes no logical sense to hold that the writers fabricated a resurrection to persuade readers to believe a lie. Of what benefit would such a fabrication have been to the writers or the readers?

And, since history and tradition tell that the apostles died martyrs' deaths (except John, who is said to have survived attempts at martyrdom, and died at an advanced age[6]), what did the writers gain by lying other than a painful and premature death?

The evidence for the resurrection of Jesus has convinced even agnostic New Testament scholar Gerd Lüdemann that the Gospel writers did not fabricate the accounts of their experiences with Jesus after His crucifixion. Lüdemann writes, "It may be taken as historically certain that Peter and the disciples had experiences after Jesus' death in which Jesus appeared to them as the risen Christ."[7] Critical scholars typically conclude that the writers entirely fabricated certain accounts in the Gospels. A prime example is the birth narratives found in Matthew and Luke. Critics contend the genealogy in Matthew cannot be reconciled with the one in Luke, that there are historical errors (e.g., dating the census to when Quirinius was governor of Syria, Luke 2:2) and there is no extra-biblical corroboration of the account of Herod's ordering the killing of the children in Bethlehem (Matthew 2:7-12).

Conservative scholars acknowledge that at least one Gospel story (called a "pericope") was added later, namely the story of the woman caught in adultery (John 7:53-8:11). The pericope does not appear in the earliest manuscripts of John, and in some manuscripts the story is found near the end of Luke's Gospel. Thus, on textual evidence,[8] the account of the woman caught in adultery was not originally part of John's Gospel. It is possible that the account is based on a true event, but there is no way to know one way or another. Regardless, the story may be evidence of an attempt by someone to embellish the story of Jesus.

If the story of the adulterous woman is admittedly an embellishment that found its way into many Greek manuscripts of John's Gospel and into most English Bibles, are the critics on to something when they contend that many of the Gospel accounts are embellished, if not fabricated? The answer is simply, "No." Critics go out on a limb if they try to extrapolate widespread embellishments in the Gospels from a single account.

Let's make two observations: First, the pericope of the woman caught in adultery was identified as an embellishment based on objective evidence, namely the absence of the account in the earliest copies of John's Gospel. Instead of mere speculation, the rejection of the account of the adulterous woman is based on verifiable manuscript data. Second, there is no similar objective evidence for excluding allegedly embellished accounts such as the birth narratives in Matthew and Luke.

Accusations that the birth narratives were fabricated are based, essentially, on the difficulties in reconciling the two genealogies, an alleged historical blunder in Luke's account,[9] and an argument from silence regarding Herod's killing of the children following the birth of Jesus. None of these allegations rise to the same level of objective textual evidence that exists for identifying and excluding the account of the adulterous woman. Thus, although a critic can argue that it is *possible* that the accounts were embellished, the evidence supporting the contention the birth narratives are fabricated falls woefully short of the evidence confirming that John 7:53-8:11 is an embellishment.

If we assume for the sake of argument that *some* embellished or even fabricated accounts made their way into the Gospels, does this disqualify the Gospels as reliable sources for *any* information about the life and teachings of Jesus? No. Critics who conclude that many of the Gospel accounts are not authentic still find "kernels of truth." An example is John Dominic Crossan, co-founder of the "Jesus Seminar," originally a group of nearly 150 liberal scholars who gathered together in the 1980s and 90s to vote on which sayings of Jesus in the Gospels they thought were authentic. Despite the Jesus Seminar's finding that less than 20% of the words attributed to Jesus were authentic[10], Crossan said, "Jesus' death by crucifixion under Pontius Pilate is as sure as anything historical can ever be."[11]

One of the problems confronting Gospel critics is what criteria to use to determine whether material in the Gospels is true or fabricated. There is no consensus, which helps illustrate the subjectivity involved in the endeavor, and how one's conclusion might be colored by assumptions and worldview.

One criterion commonly used to determine a document's historical reliability is corroboration from other sources. Later in this book we will consider examples of Gospel accounts that were disputed but later proved accurate based on recent archaeological discoveries. If, however, we accept no Gospel accounts unless corroborated by archaeological discoveries, then it seems only fair that we apply the same criterion to all ancient writings. Otherwise, the critic has employed an unfair double standard, essentially a special pleading applied to the Gospels but not to other Graeco-Roman literature of the same period.

Since allegations of embellishments and fabrications within the Gospels call into question the reliability of Gospel accounts, what evidence is there to counter these allegations? Are there affirmative clues within the Gospels that evidence a *lack* of embellishment and support the *honesty* of the accounts? Yes. These clues are known as the "criterion of embarrassment."

## CRITERION OF EMBARRASSMENT

There is consensus that the inclusion of certain types of accounts when reporting events lends credibility to the accuracy of the accounts and weighs heavily against the writers' being biased. Such accounts include those that would be embarrassing to the writers, their followers, and the heroes of their stories. John P. Meier referred to this concept as "criterion of embarrassment" in his groundbreaking work *Jesus: A Marginal Jew.*[12] Robert Funk, co-founder of the liberal "Jesus Seminar," wrote about the criterion of embarrassment as it relates to whether the New Testament contains reliable history:

Events and characterizations that would have been an embarrassment to Jesus' followers, to those forming and relating the story of his death, and yet were preserved by them, have some claim to be historical. The lack of motivation to create and transmit unflattering details is positive evidence....[13]

The legal system in America also has provisions that recognize embarrassing statements as being reliable in certain circumstances. At a trial, generally only testimony a witness offers in court is admissible. Statements made outside the courtroom are ordinarily inadmissible because they are considered "hearsay,"[14] and, therefore, unreliable. But, there are exceptions to the hearsay rule.

For example, suppose Fred sues Bob for causing damage to Fred's car. Bob claims he did not damage the car. Jim, the previous owner of Fred's car then tells Bob, outside of court, "The car was damaged when I sold it to Fred, and I told Fred to blame it on you so that you would have to pay to fix it." Even though Jim's statement was made outside of court to prove Bob's contention that he did not damage the car, Jim's statement would be admissible as an *exception* to the hearsay rule.[15] The California Evidence Code refers to this as a "declaration against interest," where a person makes a statement outside of court that is so contrary to the person's best interest that no rational person would make the statement unless it was true.

Let's apply the reasoning behind the "declaration against interest" concept to statements in the Gospels, starting with Mark's Gospel. The source of Mark's Gospel, as confirmed by Early Church Fathers Papias (ca 110) and Irenaeus (ca 180), is the recollections of the Apostle Peter as he told them to Mark. If that is the case (and few dispute that Peter was the source of Mark's Gospel), why include the account of Peter's denying Jesus? In Mark 14:53-72, Peter denies Jesus three times. The account of his denials shows cowardice, betrayal and a selfish desire to be safe and warm while Jesus is suffering humiliation, mockery, and beatings before He is sentenced to death by crucifixion. The inclusion of this passage in a Gospel that originated with Peter is unimaginable unless it is true. Peter's recalling the denials so that Mark could record them is a classic example of declarations against his interest. These are the types of statements that are legally considered reliable because they "created such a risk of making him an object of hatred, ridicule, or social disgrace in the community, that a reasonable man in his position would not have made the statement unless he believed it to be true."[16]

Many Gospel accounts serve as examples of the criterion of embarrassment. Here are 10 of the more prominent ones:

## 1. THE DISCIPLES' LACK OF STAMINA AND WILLPOWER

On the night of His betrayal, in the Garden of Gethsemane across from the East Gate that leads into the Old City of Jerusalem Jesus told His disciples, "Sit here while I go over there and pray" (Matthew 26:36). When Jesus returned, He found the disciples asleep. He then told them to "Watch and pray" (Matthew 26:41) and then went to pray a second time. When He returned, He again found the disciples sleeping (Matthew 26:43). This happened a third time, at which point Roman soldiers and Jewish leaders arrived and arrested Jesus.

Despite His admonition to "Watch and pray," the disciples slumbered, in direct disregard of their Master's words. The only plausible reason to include the details of the disciples' slumbering failures is because the account is true. It adds nothing to the prestige of Jesus, but takes away from the image of the disciples as brave, obedient followers who would do anything to please the Lord. This embarrassing event lends support to the credibility of the Gospel writers as honest reporters of facts.

## 2. THE DISCIPLES' LACK OF COURAGE

The disciples of Jesus had witnessed His betrayal and arrest in the Garden of Gethsemane, and when Jesus was crucified the next day, only one of the disciples, John, was present at Golgotha where Jesus was crucified. By contrast, three women were present as Jesus hung on a cross. These women showed tremendous courage by coming to the place where an enemy of Rome was being executed. Despite the power and authority of the Roman Empire to suspect and even punish those with allegiance to enemies of Rome like Jesus, these women came to see their Lord and Savior in His suffering and death.

This does not speak well of the courage of the disciples, who were apparently unwilling to risk appearing at the scene of Jesus' crucifixion. A fictional account would likely reverse the roles and have the men present, since men highly value recognition as courageous and loathe being seen as cowardly. As the text stands, it calls into question the disciples' bravery, an embarrassing detail that underscores the objectivity and believability of the writers.

## 3. THE DISCIPLES' LACK OF FAITH

Jesus and the disciples were aboard a boat on the Sea of Galilee when a storm suddenly arose. Jesus was sleeping, but the disciples, afraid of drowning, woke Him up, saying, "Lord, save us! We're going to drown" (Matthew 7:23-25). Jesus said to His disciples, "You of little faith, why are you so afraid?" (Matthew 7:26), and proceeded to calm the storm. The disciples were not only afraid but essentially rebuked by Jesus for having "little faith." This is another account that adds little to the prestige of Jesus whose miraculous powers are evident in numerous other passages. Instead, these verses show the weak faith and fear of the disciples. The embarrassing nature of this account is an earmark of the writer's veracity.

## 4. THE DISCIPLES' INABILITY TO UNDERSTAND JESUS

Jesus tells the disciples that He was going to be betrayed and killed but three days later rise from the dead, fulfilling everything the prophets had written (Luke 18:31-33). The disciples failed to understand what He meant, yet were afraid to ask Jesus about it (Luke 18:34). This account portrays the disciples as either unfamiliar with the Old Testament prophets, or else somewhat dimwitted (or both). Mark's account of this event adds that the disciples "were afraid to ask Him about it" (Mark 9:32). If the writer were embellishing or even making up the story why would he recount this embarrassing episode that only makes the disciples look bad? This is further evidence that the accounts are honest and straightforward as opposed to embellished.

## 5. A DISCIPLE IS STERNLY REBUKED

Three of the 12 disciples were in an "inner circle"--Peter, James and John. James became the first disciple martyred (see Acts 12:1-2). Peter and John continued as "pillars" in the Early Church, along with Jesus' brother James (Galatians 2:9). Peter was the one who answered Jesus' questions to the disciples in Caesarea Philippi, "Who do you say that I am?" (Matthew 16:15). Peter's answer, "You are the Christ, the Son of the living God," evoked a blessing from Jesus (Matthew 16:16-17). Shortly thereafter, Jesus began to explain to the disciples that He was going to suffer, be killed, and rise from the dead three days later. Peter, instead of realizing that Jesus' death was the means through which God would offer salvation to humanity, rebuked Jesus, saying, "Never, Lord! This shall never happen" (Matthew 16:22). Jesus then turned to Peter and said, "Get behind me, Satan! You are a stumbling block to Me…" (Matthew 16:23).

It is one thing for Jesus to call out the disciples for being fearful and having "little faith." It is another for Him to call one of his inner three disciples "Satan." No good reason exists to include Jesus' vituperative rebuke other than to present the account exactly as it happened. To say the passage does not make Peter look good is a colossal understatement. Using the criterion of embarrassment, this passage is strong evidence that biblical writers did not hold back from telling the truth, even when it showed a key disciple in an extremely bad light.

## 6. JESUS CONSIDERED "OUT OF HIS MIND" BY FAMILY MEMBERS

Luke's account in the Book of Acts has Judean Governor Festus using hyperbole, accusing Paul of being "out of his mind," driven insane by "great learning" (Acts 26:24). This pales in comparison to Jesus' own family accusing Him of being "out of his mind," and then coming to take charge of Him (Mark 3:21, 31). We know from the Book of Acts and Galatians that Jesus' brother James, who was likely included in the "family" that wanted to take charge of Jesus, became a central figure in the Early Church. Paul, in his first letter to the Corinthians perhaps gives us the reason for James' radical change—James was listed as one of the ones who saw the resurrected Jesus (1 Corinthians 15:7). This turn of events may soften the passage where Jesus' family thinks He is crazy, but it still serves as further example that the Gospel writers are telling the whole story, including any embarrassing details.

### 7. JESUS NOT BELIEVED BY HIS OWN BROTHERS

John tells us that even Jesus' "own brothers did not believe Him" (John 7:5). As with His family's considering Jesus out of His mind, His brothers not believing in Him adds further embarrassment. The text does not say *why* His brothers did not believe in Him, so we are left to speculate. Regardless of the reasons for their unbelief, the only explanation for including this embarrassing detail, especially in a book that was written so that people would believe, is that the writer is telling the truth. And if troubling statements are accurately recorded, then other statements can reasonably be given the benefit of the doubt and considered true unless there is competent evidence to conclude otherwise.

### 8. JESUS IS ACCUSED OF DECEPTION

In the same passage where we are told that Jesus' "own brothers did not believe Him," we are also told that some of the crowd said, "He deceives the people" (John 7:12). It is very unlikely that a writer who wanted to "spin" a story to bring the reader to a pre-determined conclusion (i.e., that Jesus is the Christ) would report that people accused Him of being a deceiver. The only explanation for sharing the crowd's accusation of deception is that the writer had the integrity to tell the whole story, good and bad.

### 9. MANY OF JESUS' FOLLOWERS ABANDONED HIM

The Gospels record many difficult sayings of Jesus. One that is understood differently in Catholic and Protestant traditions is Jesus statement in John 6:53, "unless you eat the flesh of the Son of Man and drink His blood, you have no life in you." Regardless of how one interprets this saying, the effect was significant. John tells us, "From this time many of His disciples turned back and no longer followed Him"

(John 6:66). If the Gospels were written solely as a recruiting tool, then why mention that *many* of His followers abandoned Him? How can someone who claims the Gospels are biased accounts that betray an agenda of selectively presenting facts to make Jesus look good explain John 6:66? This verse is yet another clear example that the Gospel writers present the unvarnished truth.

## 10. JESUS IS CALLED UNFLATTERING NAMES

Jesus refers to Himself metaphorically as the Bread of Life, Good Shepherd, the Resurrection and the Life, and many other metaphors. These are part of the seven "I am" statements recorded in the Gospel of John. Jesus is also referred to as "Lord," "God" and "King of Kings and Lord of Lords." But the Gospels also presents the accounts where Jesus is called unflattering names, such as "drunkard" (Matthew 11:19), "demon possessed" (Mark 3:22), and "madman" (John 10:20). He is also, by implication, under God's curse, because the Bible says, "Cursed is anyone who is hung on a tree" (Galatians 3:13, cf. Deuteronomy 21:23). Why include such unflattering references? The simplest explanation is because that is how it happened.

## CONCLUSION

The foregoing examples are not what are normally seen in fictional accounts of the lives of heroes and their followers. The raw, unvarnished truth is often not flattering, and the inclusion of such embarrassing details leads even a highly skeptical liberal theologian like Robert Funk to conclude that the accounts "have some claim to be historical" because "unflattering details" do not fit in with fiction.

The criterion of embarrassment is compelling evidence that the Gospel writers were not biased but instead honest writers who wrote what they observed or learned from eyewitnesses. Many accounts in the Gospels put the disciples in a negative light, akin to "declarations against interest" that legal rules of evidence consider to be reliable and, therefore, admissible in court as an exception to the "hearsay rule." Far from earmarks of unreliability, the numerous embarrassing accounts in the Gospels are evidence supporting the conclusion that the writers told the truth, the whole truth, and nothing but the truth in their accounts of Jesus.

# CHAPTER FOUR
# Lost Gospels?

**Issue:** Are there other "Gospels" that belong in the New Testament?

**Argument:** Only Matthew, Mark, Luke and John are the authentic Gospels, and the so-called "lost gospels" add no reliable information about Jesus' life.

## EVIDENCE IN SUPPORT OF ARGUMENT

1. Only the four "canonical" Gospels were written in the 1st century.
2. Only the canonical Gospels were written based on eyewitness accounts of the life of Jesus.
3. Only the canonical Gospels had apostolic approval.
4. The Early Church accepted only the canonical Gospels as authentic.
5. All or virtually all the non-canonical "lost gospels" were written 120 years or more after the time of Jesus.
6. Most of the lost gospels were written either as pious fiction or to promote the cult of Gnosticism.
7. The lost gospels are spurious forgeries, falsely claiming authorship by a known New Testament figure.
8. The lost gospels do not add a single verifiable new fact about the ministry of Jesus.
9. The lost gospels are championed by popular writers and television networks to sell books and attract television viewers.
10. The "lost gospels" are neither lost, nor Gospels. They were known and rejected by the Early Church for being spurious and heretical.

## STRAINING OUT GNATS WHILE SWALLOWING CAMELS

*"More than 80 gospels were considered for the New Testament, and yet only a relative few were chosen for inclusion — Matthew,*

*Mark, Luke and John among them.*" Dan Brown, *The Da Vinci Code,* p. 231

"The Gospel of Judas Iscariot: World Exclusive 'Greatest Archaeological Discovery of all Time' Threat to 2,000 Years of Christian Teaching." Daily Mail headline, April 2006

From time to time a television show or book will purport to present "lost words of Jesus" or "secret teachings of Jesus." The claim is made that secrets about the life and teachings of Jesus are contained in recently-discovered ancient writings not found in the canonical Gospels of Matthew, Mark, Luke, and John. Some of these writings call themselves "gospels," and their proponents contend they provide new details about the historical Jesus. They also typically assert that these are "lost gospels" that contain truth suppressed by the Church because this newly-discovered material contradicts the content of the canonical Gospels (i.e., Gospels accepted by the Church).

A lay person's eyes may glaze over trying to separate the wheat from the sensational chaff of the so-called "lost gospels." This helps explain why a fiction writer like Dan Brown, author of the infamous *Da Vinci Code* novel found a way to cash in by misrepresenting facts and spinning yarns based on half-truths and innuendos.

The various early written accounts of Jesus that are not part of the New Testament canon are referred to as "non-canonical gospels" or "extra-biblical gospels."[1] Many of these writings were mentioned by early Christian writers, but no copies were known to have survived until the past 120 years when fragments and an occasional complete copy of some of these works were discovered in the dry sands of Egypt. The origin of these non-canonical "gospels" is murky. Their authors are unknown, and their agenda, if it can be determined from the content, often appears to be the creation of a fictional Jesus to advance a point of view not supported by the traditional Gospels.

The debate continues as to whether the "lost gospels" add *any* reliable facts about the life of Jesus, and whether they should even be called "gospels." Like the breakfast cereal *Grape Nuts*, which is neither grapes nor nuts, the evidence supports the conclusion that these non-canonical writings are neither "lost" nor "gospels." Because of their fanciful or heretical content, many of these writings were likely discarded in the early centuries, only to be rediscovered in modern times and misused by promoters of baseless new theories about Jesus.

## EXAMPLES OF "LOST GOSPELS"

The so-called "lost gospels" include the Gospel of Judas, Gospel of Peter, Gospel of Thomas, Gospel of Phillip, Gospel of Truth, Gospel of the Egyptians, Infancy Gospel of Thomas, Gospel of Mary Magdalene, Gospel of Nicodemus, Gospel of Josephus, Gospel of James, *ad infinitum, ad nauseum.*

How does one know whether the four canonical Gospels are the only true accounts of the life and teachings of Jesus, or even if they are true accounts? Do these extra-biblical texts provide any new facts regarding the life and teachings of Jesus?

As former atheist and Christian apologist C. S. Lewis said, "A man does not call a line crooked unless he has some idea of a straight line." To properly understand the nature of the "lost gospels," we need to have a standard by which to evaluate them. That standard is the canonical Gospels of Matthew, Mark, Luke, and John, and the question is, "How do the 'lost gospels' compare to the Gospels in terms of when they were written, who wrote them, and whether they provide new information about the life and teachings of Jesus?"

## THE CANONICAL GOSPELS

In Chapter Two ("Who Wrote the Gospels?") we considered an abundance of evidence that the Gospels of Matthew, Mark, Luke, and John came from Apostles (Matthew, John) and men connected to the Apostles (Mark writing the recollections of the Apostle Peter and Luke, a companion of Paul, writing as an investigative journalist). We have presented the external evidence (e.g., quotes from 2nd century Church Fathers Papias and Irenaeus; the exclusive use of the canonical Gospels in Tatian's *Diatessaron*) and internal evidence and found there are *no* existing traditions of anyone other than Matthew, Mark, Luke, and John as the writers of our four Gospels.

The New Testament "canon" refers to those 27 books that the historic Christian Church, and its current three branches (Catholic, Protestant, Orthodox), consider authoritative. A "canon" is a standard or ruler by which other things are judged (i.e., C. S. Lewis' straight line). A complete discussion of the canonicity of the 27 New Testament books is beyond the scope of this book, but several recent books deftly cover the issue of canonicity, including addressing the main questions about the canon.[2]

We need to address the issue of non-canonical, "lost gospels" on several levels. First, the witness of the Early Church plays an important role. Substantial evidence for the authenticity of solely the four Gospels comes from the surviving writings of Early Church Fathers and the fact that the Early Church accepted only Matthew, Mark, Luke, and John as authoritative. Anyone advocating for other "gospels" as reliable biographies of Jesus must bear the burden of explaining how the Early Church failed to recognize any other accounts of His life and teachings as accurate and authentic.

Second, the date of "lost gospels" must be determined. Any so-called "lost gospels" written in the mid-2nd century or later cannot be eyewitness accounts or even primary source accounts that had access to eyewitnesses.

Third, if a "lost gospel" bears the name of an Apostle or known New Testament figure (e.g., Nicodemus), and the evidence confirms that the "lost gospel" was not written by the Apostle or New Testament figure, then the writing is a "forgery."[3]

Fourth, if a "lost gospel" contradicts the testimony of reliable sources about the life and teachings of Jesus and His followers, then any claim to authenticity fails unless somehow the claimant can adduce sufficient evidence to show that the known and accepted facts about Jesus are wrong.

Fifth, the nature of "lost gospels" must be scrutinized to see whether they have earmarks of being ancient biographies or instead are more likely pious fiction and Gnostic[4] alterations rather than historical accounts.

## WITNESS OF THE EARLY CHURCH

There appears to have been rapid and virtually unanimous acceptance of 20 of the 27 New Testament books, including all four Gospels.[5] Seven New Testament books had some detractors before they were finally accepted as canonical.[6] Several popular writings circulated among early Christians but were not included in the New Testament canon.[7] Finally, there were obvious forgeries, usually writings that falsely used the name of a New Testament figure in hopes of gaining acceptance.[8] The Early Church's acceptance of the four Gospels and later ratification by Church Councils[9] in the 4th century created the benchmark by which any additional candidates must be judged.

## THE DATE, AUTHORSHIP AND CONTENT OF THE "LOST GOSPELS"

### DATE OF THE "LOST GOSPELS"

Although a biography written 100 years or more after someone died can still contain truth about the person, the more remote in time an ancient biography is from the subject person's life, the greater the question of accuracy. For later written biographies, we must address certain foundational questions, such as who the biographer is and what are the biographer's sources. An anonymous biographer or one whose sources are unknown may still have kernels of truth, but in such a case it is essential to confirm the accounts from known and accepted sources before putting much credence in the anonymously written biography.

One of the factors that militates against authenticity and reliability of the "lost gospels" is their dates of composition. What these documents have in common, among other factors, is that they were likely written 120 years or more *after* the time of Jesus.[10] This fact alone excludes the "lost gospels" from serious consideration as authentic sources for the life of Jesus.

### "LOST GOSPELS" AS FORGERIES

Since any "gospel" written 120 years or more after the time of Jesus could not have been written by one of the Apostles or an eyewitness to Jesus' life, "lost gospels" that bear the names of New Testament figures as their writers are obvious forgeries. The canonical Gospels, regardless of whether one accepts their traditional authorship or considers them "anonymous," cannot be forgeries, because there is no specific claim of authorship within their texts. It was not uncommon in ancient times for a writer to add the name of a known person in order to get the writing accepted, e.g., *Homeric Hymns* were not written by Homer. Thus, the 2nd century writings in names of New Testament figures such as Phillip, Peter, Thomas, etc., are not unusual for that era.

## CONSISTENCY OF "LOST GOSPELS" WITH THE KNOWN LIFE AND SAYINGS OF JESUS

Another earmark of many of the "lost gospels," especially those called "Infancy Gospels," is the pattern of presenting events from Jesus' "silent years." The canonical Gospels cover events about Jesus from birth to age two, then one event (teaching in the Temple) at age 12, then nothing until Jesus reaches age 30. Many of the "lost gospels" try to fill in the silent years and some also add details about Mary and Joseph.

If the "lost gospels" merely embellished accounts of Jesus, the Early Church might have ignored them, but some present false teachings, contradicting the canonical Gospels. Inconsistency with the historical Gospels is another criterion for exposing and rejecting the lost gospels as being authentic.

## EARMARKS SUGGESTING MANY "LOST GOSPELS" WERE WRITTEN AS PIOUS FICTION

Since the canonical Gospels detail the events of Jesus' three-year ministry (age 30-33), the "lost gospels" typically do not try to add to the established Gospel record of Jesus' miracles for those years.[11] Instead, there are "sayings gospels" that claim to provide "secret conversations" between Jesus and others (e.g., Thomas and Mary—see below under "Significant 'Lost Gospels'") and several "infancy gospels" that provide entertaining stories about Jesus as a child. Many of the infancy gospels and apocryphal acts of Paul and others appear to be written as a substitute for heathen novels. A genre of religious fiction that was produced at that time to displace immoral pagan literature and promote piety, as well as to present the authors' views of Christian truth.[12] One vivid example is contained in the *Acts of Paul* in which Paul baptizes a talking lion.[13]

The "infancy gospels" include:

**Infancy Gospel of Thomas**, in which Jesus makes birds from mud and breathes life into them, and does other assorted miracles, including malevolent ones. Irenaeus knew about and quoted from this writing in the late 2nd century (ca 185-195).[14] A later Latin version of the writing attributes it to "Thomas the

Israelite." Origen (ca 230) and Hippolytus of Rome (ca 215) both refer to a *Gospel of Thomas* which is probably a reference to the *Infancy Gospel of Thomas* rather than to the *Gospel of Thomas* found in Egypt at Oxyrhynchus and Nag Hammadi.

*Infancy Gospel of James,* also known as the *Gospel of James* and *Protoevangelium of James,* appears to have been written, at the earliest, in the mid-2nd century.[15] It deals more with Mary, the mother of Jesus, than with Jesus Himself, and is the oldest source for Mary's being a virgin both before and after the birth of Jesus (the Roman Catholic doctrine of the "perpetual virginity of Mary").

*Syriac Infancy Gospel* (also known as *Arabic Infancy Gospel*) has baby Jesus talking to Mary from His cradle, asserting that He is "the Son of God." This 6th century (ca) writing has a parallel in the Qur'an, Sura 19:29-34,[16] in which Jesus also engages in a theological discussion while a baby in His cradle. The existence in the Qur'an of a direct parallel to a spurious infancy gospel does not bode well for the reliability of the Qur'an as an historical source for the life of Jesus.

*Infancy Gospel of Matthew,* also known as *Pseudo-Matthew* and *The Book About the Origin of the Blessed Mary and the Childhood of the Savior,* was likely written after the year 600. The work appears to be a re-write of the *Infancy Gospel of James* and the *Infancy Gospel of Thomas,* with several new embellishments about Mary and Joseph.

## EARMARKS SUGGESTING MANY "LOST GOSPELS" WERE WRITTEN TO PROMOTE GNOSTIC BELIEFS

Some of the so-called "lost gospels" have Jesus uttering new sayings (and are sometimes called "sayings gospels," e.g., *Gospel of Thomas*—see below). Some of these sayings are modifications of Jesus' words in the canonical Gospels, and some are new and often bizarre statements that typically promote the 2nd century heresy of Gnosticism. For example, Gnosticism claimed special insight into matters that was unavailable to the masses. Hence, since the *Gospel of Thomas* begins by stating it contains the "hidden words" of Jesus, and since its manuscripts were found in troves of other Gnostic writings, it is reasonable to conclude that *Thomas* is a Gnostic work. The same reasoning applies to the *Gospel of Judas* (see below), which claims to be the "secret account" of what Jesus revealed to Judas.

## EARMARKS OF JEWISH-CHRISTIAN "LOST GOSPELS"

None of the "lost gospels" in the "Jewish-Christian" category still exist. The content of these writings is known only from citations or summaries from later Christian writers such as Clement of Alexandria (ca 200), Eusebius (ca 340), Cyril of Jerusalem (ca 350), and Jerome (ca 400). The common thread in these Jewish-Christian writings is the need for Jewish converts to Christianity to continue observing the law and Jewish customs. This category includes:

*Gospel of Hebrews* is the only gospel in this category that early Christian writers (e.g., Clement of Alexandria, Jerome, Eusebius) refer to by name. Eusebius listed *Gospel of Hebrews* as *antilegomena* (literally "spoken against"), adding that Hegesippus (ca 180) was familiar with it, and used it as a source for his work *Memoirs*,[17] which is lost other than a few citations from Eusebius. Craig Evans dates *Gospel of Hebrews* to about 140.[18]

*Gospel of the Ebionites* is known only through seven citations from Epiphanius of Salamis (ca 390), which he incorrectly thought to be a Hebrew gospel derived from the authentic *Gospel of Matthew.* The Ebionites were a Jewish-Christian sect who accepted that Jesus was the Messiah but denied His deity and advocated keeping the law and Jewish customs. The name *Gospel of the Ebionites* was not used by the Early Church, but is used today to distinguish it from any Hebrew gospel based on the canonical *Matthew.* Evans dates *Ebionites* to about 120.[19]

*Gospel of the Nazarenes* is also known only from a few citations from early Christian writers, and is used to distinguish the document behind these citations from the *Gospel of Hebrews* and the *Gospel of the Ebionites.* Evans dates this "lost gospel" to about 120.[20]

*Gospel of the Egyptians*, also referred to as *Greek Gospel of the Egyptians*, is known from citations by Clement of Alexandria (ca 200) and Hippolytus (ca 210). It likely was a "sayings" gospel, and advocated celibacy in a dialogue between Salome and Jesus. The title *Gospel of the Egyptians* is taken from the presumed opening line of the text. Evans dates it to about 120.[21] This gospel is to be distinguished from a Coptic *Gospel of Egyptians* (also called *Holy Book of the Great Invisible* Spirit), a Gnostic text discovered at Nag Hammadi in 1945.

## HOW MUCH HISTORICAL TRUTH DO THE LOST GOSPELS ADD TO THE LIFE OF JESUS?

As to how much reliable new material the "lost gospels" add to the life and teachings of Jesus, scholars conclude, essentially, "none." Biblical scholar Raymond Brown, addressing the Gnostic Gospels found at Nag Hammadi, Egypt, says that from them "we learn not a single verifiable new fact about the historical Jesus' ministry, and only a few new sayings that might possibly have been his."[22] Andrew Gregory concludes, "the non-canonical gospels offer little evidence about the historical Jesus."[23] Thus, for anyone who wants to find out about the historical Jesus, the canonical Gospels remain the most, if not only, reliable sources.

## SIGNIFICANT "LOST GOSPELS"

### GOSPEL OF THOMAS

> Saying 114: Simon Peter said to him, Let Mary leave us, for women are not worthy of life. Jesus said, I myself shall lead her in order to make her male, so that she too may become a living spirit resembling you males. For every woman who will make herself male will enter the kingdom of heaven.

Around 1896, archaeologists Bernard Grenfell and Arthur Hunt began discovering thousands of fragments of ancient documents in a garbage dump near Oxyrhynchus, Egypt. Among the fragments were three in the Greek language that contained sayings attributed to Jesus. These fragments were believed to all be portions of a larger work. It was not until 1945, when another trove of ancient documents was discovered near the Egyptian town of Nag Hammadi, that scholars realized the fragments from Oxyrhynchus were part of a document known in the 4th century as the *Gospel of Thomas*.

The Nag Hammadi *Gospel of Thomas*, written in Coptic, begins, "These are the hidden words that the living Jesus spoke and Didymus

Judas Thomas wrote them down," followed by 114 sayings ("logia") attributed to Jesus. The manuscript ends with the words, "The Gospel According to Thomas." Nearly half the sayings are similar to Jesus' sayings found in the canonical Gospels, with the remainder being closer to the Gnostic tradition. The document purports to contain the "secret" or "hidden" teachings of Jesus that He taught privately to Thomas and the other disciples.

The *Gospel of Thomas* contains no narrative (e.g., "Jesus and the disciples went from Galilee to Jerusalem"). Because most of the other documents found at Nag Hammadi were Gnostic texts, most scholars assume that the *Gospel of Thomas* was compiled by Gnostics.[24] Church historian Eusebius of Caesarea (ca 325) included the *Gospel of Thomas* among a group of books he believed to be not only spurious, but the fictions of heretics.[25]

Scholars debate when the *Gospel of Thomas* was originally written. The Coptic manuscript found at Nag Hammadi (part of a leather book, or *codex*), was likely written around 325.[26] The Greek fragments found at Oxyrhynchus date at least as early as the Coptic manuscript, with the possibility that one of the fragments was copied as early as A.D. 200.[27] Scholars concede that *Thomas* could have been written as early as A.D. 150 but "the evidence strongly suggests that *Thomas* was not composed before A.D. 175 or 180.[28]

A few scholars[29] contend that *Thomas* contains "pre-synoptic tradition," meaning some material comes from a time before Matthew, Mark and Luke were written. New Testament scholar Craig A. Evans makes a strong case against *Thomas* being a primitive account, independent of the canonical Gospels. Evans sets forth four reasons why *Thomas* is a late writing:

(1) *Thomas* knows many of the New Testament writings.

(2) *Thomas* contains Gospel materials that scholars regard as late.

(3) *Thomas* reflects later editing in the Gospels.

(4) *Thomas* shows familiarity with traditions distinctive to Eastern, Syrian Christianity traditions that did not emerge before the middle of the second century.[30]

Despite some theories that contend *Thomas* gives us early teachings of Jesus and serves as a source for the historical Jesus, there is no evidence that the *Gospel of Thomas* is authentic (i.e., written by Thomas the disciple), that it was known in the 1st century, or and that it was ever considered authentic by the Early Church. Instead, *Thomas* should be considered a mid-to-late 2nd century Gnostic work that has essentially no value as a supplemental source of the life and teachings of Jesus.

## GOSPEL OF JUDAS

Irenaeus, writing about 180, references a *Gospel of Judas*, calling it "a fictitious history."[31] The next reference to this spurious gospel is from Epiphanius, a 4th century monk. The *Gospel of Judas* is known from only one papyrus copy, written in Coptic, which was discovered in 1978 in a cave in the village of Ambar, north of Al Minya, Egypt.[32] The manuscript, which contains approximately 85% of the original text, has been dated to around the year A.D. 300.[33]

*Gospel of Judas* is essentially a purported conversation between Jesus and Judas Iscariot, who is uniquely chosen to receive Jesus' deepest teachings because he is Jesus' greatest disciple. The document begins, "The secret account of the revelation that Jesus spoke in conversation with Judas Iscariot."

The *Gospel of Judas* was originally thought to make Judas out to be a hero, recasting his efforts as essential to allowing Jesus to accomplish His sacrificial mission. This strange tendency to turn a biblical villain into a hero was the practice of a group Irenaeus called the Cainites. According to Cainite thinking, anyone the evil god hates-- e.g., Cain, Esau, Sodomites and Judas—must actually be a good person.

The idea of Judas as a hero prompted the National Geographic Society to sensationalize their published release of a translation of the *Gospel of Judas* in 2006, concurrent with a television special, "The Gospel of Judas: The Lost Version of Christ's Betrayal," which aired on the National Geographic Channel in April, 2006.

Scholars Bart Ehrman and Elaine Pagels, who previously had found receptive audiences for their books about early texts that challenged traditional Christianity, jumped on the bandwagon and wrote their own accounts of the *Gospel of Judas*. Ehrman's *The Last Gospel of*

*Judas Iscariot* and Pagels' *Reading Judas* (written with Karen King) perpetuated National Geographic's theme of Judas as a hero. Ehrman also mirrored some of National Geographic's hype in an essay, writing that the *Gospel of Judas* "...will open up new vistas for understanding Jesus and the religious movement he founded."[34]

However, once scholars were able to access legible copies of the text of the *Gospel of Judas* (which previously had been carefully controlled by National Geographic and its team of translators), several prominent Coptic scholars found that mistranslations by the National Geographic team created the "Judas as a hero" narrative, when, in fact, a proper translation sees Judas as evil, condemned, and denied Heaven, similar to his fate in the canonical Gospels.[35] That narrative, of course, does not sell books or induce people to watch a television special.

Further study of the *Gospel of Judas* led scholars to a different conclusion from that of National Geographic, Ehrman and Pagels. These studies found the author of the *Gospel of Judas* affiliated with Sethian Gnostic teachings.[36] In Sethian Gnosticism, the creator-god of the Old Testament was an *Archon,* a demonic trickster god opposed to the transcendent God the Gnostics worshiped. In the *Gospel of Judas* Jesus calls Judas the "Thirteenth Demon," the same title given to the chief *Archon.* Thus, Judas is identified with the chief demon that tries to lead people astray and keep them from knowledge of the true, transcendent God. The *Gospel of Judas* also appears to be a means for Gnostic Christians to challenge, even oppose, apostolic Christians, whom Sethian Gnostics did not consider to be real Christians.[37]

Aside from any entertainment value, scholars find *no* historical value in the *Gospel of Judas* for understanding either Judas or Jesus.[38]

## GOSPEL OF TRUTH

The *Gospel of Truth* is a mid-2nd century Gnostic text known to Irenaeus (ca 180), who denounced it[39] as being a heretical work of disciples of Valentinus (ca 100-160), a Gnostic theologian. All traces of the *Gospel of Truth* vanished until a Copic text was discovered at Nag Hammadi in 1945. In keeping with the Gnostic aspiration for knowledge, this gospel presents Jesus as having been sent down to earth to remove ignorance. Because the style is more poetic, many consider *Gospel of Truth* as a commentary on the Gospels rather than a gospel that attempts to add to the life and teachings of Jesus.

## GOSPEL OF PETER

The *Gospel of Peter* is another non-canonical gospel that was lost for centuries but believed to have been rediscovered in modern times. It was mentioned by Origen (ca 230) and Eusebius (ca 330). Church historian Eusebius references a letter by Serapion (ca 190-200) that denounces *Gospel of Peter* for seemingly encouraging Christians to embrace the error of *docetism*.[40] Origen's reference to the *Gospel of Peter* may refer to a different writing.

What scholars call the *Gospel of Peter* was found in 1886 in Akhmim, Egypt, about 60 miles north of Nag Hammadi. The manuscript dates to about the 8th century and is fragmentary, missing the beginning and ending. Eusebius notes the existence of certain works attributed to the Apostle Peter, but states that only the canonical book of First Peter was authentic. He specifically mentions that the *Gospel of Peter* was rejected by the Church, referencing "writings that are put forward by heretics under the name of the apostles containing Gospels such as those of Peter, and Thomas, and Matthias, and some others besides."[41] Before assuming that the Akhmim fragment is the *Gospel of Peter* referenced by Serapion and Eusebius, it is worth noting that scholars such as Craig Evans see substantial weakness in the identification of the Akhmim fragment with the 2nd century *Gospel of Peter*.[42]

The *Gospel of Peter* has some unusual features, such as a cross that talks and angels whose heads reach into the clouds. Despite some who suggest the Akhmim fragment is from a tradition that pre-dates the canonical Gospels and may have even been a source for the canonical Gospels,[43] this view does not appear to hold sway among most scholars, who see the fragment as a 2nd century "pastiche of traditions from the canonical Gospels, recycled through the memory and lively imagination of Christians who have heard the Gospels read and preached upon many a time."[44]

## GOSPEL OF MARY

About half of the original text of the *Gospel of Mary* exists in three fragments. The first fragment was discovered in 1896 in Akhmim, as part of a codex[42] containing other writings. The original date of writing is uncertain, but was written no earlier than the mid-2nd century.[45] The *Gospel of Mary* purports to be an account in which Mary Magdalene informs the disciples of what Jesus told her, which is at odds with what Jesus had told them. Peter and Andrew are dubious, which causes Mary to weep and Levi to come to her aid. At one point the text reads, "Sister, we know that you were much loved by the Savior, as no other woman."

This text has been used by fiction writers and sensationalistic journalists to suggest that Jesus and Mary were lovers and may even have been married. This fabrication usually also employs the *Gospel of Philip* (see below) to make the case for a married Jesus. Whether the *Gospel of Mary* was an early effort designed to increase the role of women in the Church is debatable. There is no basis to consider anything in the *Gospel of Mary* as coming from the historical Jesus or Mary Magdalene.[46]

## GOSPEL OF PHILIP

A 3rd century Gnostic text, the *Gospel of Philip* was discovered near Nag Hammadi, Egypt in 1945. It was bound together in the same codex that contained the *Gospel of Thomas*. Only 17 sayings of Jesus occur in the entire writing, and nine of these are modifications of Jesus' words in the canonical Gospels. The content includes two passages relating to Mary Magdalene, calling her Jesus' "companion," a Coptic variant of the Greek *koinonos*, which is used in the Bible to connote a "companion in the faith" (Philemon 17), a fellow-worker in the Gospel (2 Corinthians 8:23), and, rarely, a partner who is a spouse (Malachi 2:14 in the LXX[47]). Of course, translating the *koinonos* as "fellow-worker" does not sell books or create interest in television specials. Thus, the improbable conclusion that Mary Magdalene is called the "spouse" of Jesus" became the focal point of articles, books and television "specials" about the Gospel of Philip and its supposed earth-shaking implications.

The passage that sensationalists fixate on requires a fertile imagination to arrive at their conclusions. Translated into English, it reads as follows, including the gaps in the manuscript:

And the companion of the [              ] Mary Magdalene.
[              ] her more than [      ] the disciples    [              ]
kiss her [     ] on her [      ].

There is no credible reason to conclude that the *Gospel of Philip* intends to say that Jesus and Mary Magdalene were lovers or were married. The *Gospel of Philip* also directly attacks teachings in the canonical Gospels, such as the virgin birth of Jesus.[48] Thus, no logical reason exists for anyone to accept anything within the *Gospel of Philip* as being new historical information about Jesus or Mary Magdalene.

## OTHER "LOST GOSPELS"

There are other "lost gospels" that purport to add new details to the life and teachings of Jesus or to come from traditions that pre-date the canonical Gospels (e.g., *Egerton Gospel*,[49] *Secret Gospel of Mark*,[50] *Pistis Sophia*[51]). Other "lost gospels" make even more bizarre, purely metaphysical claims without any historical or textual support (e.g., *Aquarian Gospel*[52]). One could spend a lifetime tracking down "lost gospel" claims, but suffice to say that with a wealth of reliable (by recognized standards) historical evidence for the life and teachings of Jesus from the canonical Gospels, the burden is on those claiming any "lost gospels" provide new information that is historically credible.[53]

## CONCLUSION

No early Christian traditions identify anyone other than Matthew, Mark, Luke, and John as the writers of the authentic biographies of Jesus. No strong case can be made for any non-canonical gospels containing traditions that predate the canonical Gospels, and no case can be made for the "lost gospels" adding anything to our knowledge of the life and teachings of Jesus. Though the Gospel of John acknowledges it is an edited account of Jesus life and teachings (John 21:25), there is no reason to believe that any of the lost gospels provide us with accurate historical accounts that were omitted from the canonical Gospels. Therefore, what we reliably know about the historical Jesus is what is found in the Gospels of Matthew, Mark, Luke and John.

# CHAPTER FIVE
# Are the Gospels the Same Today as When Originally Written?

Issue:      Has the text of the Gospels changed over time from their original wording?

Argument:   The original manuscripts ("autographs") of the Gospels are missing, but their wording can be reconstructed with confidence from existing copies because of the wealth of available evidence.

## EVIDENCE IN SUPPORT OF ARGUMENT

1. The originals of all writings of antiquity are missing, requiring their original text to be reconstructed from existing copies, called "manuscripts."

2. Although the original text of ancient Greek and Roman writings are reconstructed from a handful of copies written nearly 1,000 years after the original writings, rarely, if ever, is the text of these writings challenged based on the meager amount of manuscript evidence.

3. Fragments of the Gospels exist that were copied as close as 30-40 years from the time of the original writing, and complete copies exist that were copied 100-150 years after the original writing.

4. The Manuscript Comparison Factor demonstrates that for the New Testament has three times more manuscript evidence in the first 300 years after its writing than for the average Graeco-Roman literature in the first 1,000 years after its writing.

5. If the reliability of the Gospels is challenged on textual grounds, then all classical antiquity must be rejected, because no document of the ancient world is as well attested by manuscript evidence.

6. 99% of the variations between existing Gospel manuscripts are easily resolved, and the original text of the Gospels can be reconstructed with better than 99% certainty.

## HAVE THE GOSPELS BEEN CHANGED FROM WHAT THEY ORIGINALLY SAID?

One of the most common criticisms of the New Testament, especially the Gospels, is that what we have today is not the same as what was originally written. Critics often claim that the Gospels have been copied and recopied, translated and re-translated, edited, altered and rewritten. A layperson has little opportunity to scrutinize such claims in light of current scholarship. Most of these criticisms do not come from reputable scholars who specialize in the field of analyzing ancient texts. Instead, claims that the Gospels today are much different from the original versions typically come from writers of fiction or sensationalistic writers who know that books about Jesus, especially those out of the "mainstream," have a good chance of becoming popular. It is a statement on human nature that the more sensational and outlandish the claims, the greater the chance the book will be noticed and purchased. The 1982 book, *Holy Blood, Holy Grail,* is a prime example:

> *When Constantine commissioned new versions of these documents, it enabled the custodians of orthodoxy to revise, edit, and rewrite their material as they saw fit, in accordance with their tenets. It was at this point that most of the crucial alterations in the New Testament were probably made and Jesus assumed the unique status he has enjoyed ever since. The importance of Constantine's commission must not be underestimated. Of the five thousand early manuscript versions of the New Testament, not one predates the fourth century. The New Testament as it exists today is essentially a product of fourth-century editors and writers— custodians of orthodoxy, "adherents of the message," with vested interests to protect.* [1]

## MISSING ORIGINALS

Two indisputable facts exist that demand examination of the existing handwritten copies of the Gospels: (1) None of the original documents ("autographs") are known to exist, and (2) the existing copies differ from one another in many places.[2] Even if we make the case that the Gospels were written close to the events they describe, by eyewitnesses (or somehow connected to the eyewitnesses), without bias, what we today call the "Gospels" may still be unreliable if the original wording has been altered.

To determine the original wording of the Gospels or any document when the original is unknown (e.g., lost, missing, destroyed, worn out), scholars examine the existing ("extant") copies. Any variation between the copies ("variant readings," i.e., scribal errors or intentional changes to the original text) are evaluated by established principles, called "canons"[3] to determine the original text. This process is called *textual criticism*, the art and science of examining copies to reconstruct the original wording of literature where the autograph is unknown.[4]

Anyone who carefully studies the Gospels and the entire New Testament knows that even without the autographs, there exists an "embarrassing wealth" of handwritten copies ("manuscripts") of the Gospels available for reconstructing the original wording. This wealth includes manuscripts that were copied much closer in time to when the originals were written than any other work of ancient literature, and the number of extant copies compared to other writings of antiquity. The tools used to reconstruct the original text of the Gospels include Greek manuscripts, translations of the Gospels into other languages (e.g., Latin) called "versions," and writings of post-apostolic Church Fathers.

## CRITERION OF COMPARISON

Textual criticism of any literature, whether the Gospels, ancient Graeco-Roman literature, or even Shakespeare, follows accepted practices of textual analysis and reconstruction. Honest investigators will reject any attempt at a "special pleading" that requires a different standard of evaluation for the Gospels than for any other ancient literature. They will also use the same principles to determine the textual reliability of the Gospels that are used to determine textual reliability of all other ancient texts.

When scholars talk about the "wealth" of documents available to determine the original wording of the Gospels, the "wealth" is a reference to how many manuscripts exist and when they were copied in relation to the original writing *compared to other literature of the same period.* In other words, when examining Graeco-Roman literature from the time of the Gospels, one should ask: (1) How many copies of the works of contemporary writers such as Jewish historian Flavius Josephus (ca 95) and Roman historian Cornelius Tacitus (ca 110) are in existence? (2) How many years after the original version of the work were the oldest existing copies written? This information is then compared to the Gospels to assess their manuscript evidence in relation to works whose texts are rarely, if ever, questioned. I will henceforth refer to this comparison as the "Manuscript Comparison Factor."[5]

## MANUSCRIPT COMPARISON FACTOR AS A DEMONSTRATION OF TEXTUAL RELIABILITY

To properly address whether our handwritten copies of the Gospels are reliable, we must first define "reliability." In the context of applying the Manuscript Comparison Factor, "reliability" means the original wording of the Gospels can reasonably be found in existing manuscripts. If the original wording can reasonably be found in existing copies, this finding resolves the issue of whether the original text has been lost or changed. In other words, "reliability" here means *textual reliability*, that is, the confidence that what exists today essentially reflects what was originally written. This is different from both *historical reliability*, which deals with whether the information contained in a document is historically true, and *authenticity*, which determines whether a document is a forgery.

Since "reliability" means a manuscript has textual fidelity to the original is what is meant by "reliability," does reliability then depend on the number of Gospel manuscripts and the time interval between the original and the earliest copy? Not necessarily. The Manuscript Comparison factor does not completely resolve whether copies of the Gospels are faithful to the original text. We will need more information to make an affirmative case for the text of the Gospels.

To illustrate the limitations of what the Manuscript Comparison factor can show, assume the autograph (original document) of an ancient work is missing, but a copy exists that was made 50 years after the original. Regardless of the gap between the original writing and the oldest existing copy, and regardless of the number of extant copies, poor copying by scribes or intentional changes at any point of the transmission ("copying") of the text means the existing copy falls short of being an exact replica of the original.

In the above illustration, there is no way of knowing whether the copy made 50 years after the original was copied directly from the original, or from copies of copies of copies several generations removed from the original. Having copies that were made close in time to the original writing is a factor in assessing textual reliability, since a shorter gap between original writing and the oldest copy tends to limit the number of generations of copies, which in turn, suggests fewer variations from the original. In other words, copies of copies typically have fewer changes than copies of copies of copies of copies, since each generation of copying adds changes to the original text. Therefore, a shorter time between original writing and oldest copy is a positive factor when arguing that the copy accurately reflects the original text.

## SUMMARY OF NEW TESTAMENT MANUSCRIPT EVIDENCE COMPARED TO OTHER ANCIENT WRITINGS

New Testament manuscripts as well as copies of other writings of antiquity continue to be discovered, so even updated figures are subject to revision. The current number of New Testament Greek manuscripts is currently approaching 5,900,[6] most of which contain one or more of the Gospels, plus roughly 20,000 copies of versions (translations from the Greek), and close to 20,000 citations of the Gospels alone from Church Fathers in the 2nd through 4th centuries. When compared to other popular works of antiquity, the results are telling. There are around 1,800 manuscripts of Homer's *Iliad*, 33 manuscripts of Roman historian Tacitus (ca A.D. 110), 251 copies of Caesar's *Gallic Wars* (ca 50 B.C.). The oldest copy of Tacitus is from A.D. 850, and the oldest copy of Caesar dates around A.D. 900.[7] The oldest confirmed New Testament fragment dates to A.D. 125, with complete copies of New Testament books from the mid-to-late 2nd century.[8]

| | Written | Oldest Copy/Frag | No. of Copies |
|---|---|---|---|
| Homer *Illiad* | 900 B.C. | 500 B.C. | 1,800 |
| Caesar *Gallic Wars* | 50 B.C. | A.D. 900 | 251 |
| Tacitus *Annals* | A.D. 110 | A.D. 850 | 33 |
| New Testament | A.D. 40-95 | A.D. 125 | 25,000 |

## CONTRIBUTION OF TEXTUAL CRITICISM TO THE ISSUE OF THE GOSPELS' TEXTUAL RELIABILITY

Is the Manuscript Comparison Factor relevant to substantiate the textual reliability of the Gospels and of the entire New Testament? Yes, it is relevant, but not conclusive. It is reasonable to accept that the shorter the time between the original writing and the oldest copy, the less chance the original text has been lost. Further, although having thousands of manuscripts inevitably means more variations to resolve than if there were only a dozen existing manuscripts, the wealth of manuscripts can also mean there is a clearer picture of textual transmission. This proves to be the case with the New Testament, as many textual scholars conclude that more than 99% of the original New Testament text can be ascertained with certainty, owing mainly to the wealth of evidence available for reconstructing the original wording and the relative consistency of the transmission process.[9] As F. F. Bruce writes:

> Fortunately, if the great number of [manuscripts] increases the number of scribal errors, it increases proportionately the means of correcting such errors, so that the margin of doubt left in the process of recovering the exact original wording is not so large as might be feared; it is in truth remarkably small.[10]

In short, the wealth of New Testament manuscript evidence, together with the application of textual criticism to remove variations results in a very high level of confidence that the original text can reasonably be determined. See below, "The Significance of Variations in the New Testament Manuscripts."

## EVIDENCE THAT NONE OF THE ORIGINAL TEXT OF THE GOSPELS HAS BEEN LOST

Manuscript evidence for the Gospels includes complete copies of books that were made around 100 years or so after the original writings. Although this may sound like a long time, when compared to other works of antiquity, it is minuscule. More than 70 years ago Sir Frederick Kenyon, Principal Librarian of the British Museum, summarized this point: "The interval, then, between the dates of original composition and the earliest extant evidence becomes so small as to be in fact negligible."[11] Since Kenyon made his statement, many more 2nd and 3rd century manuscripts of the Gospels have been discovered.

The earliest existing copies of the Gospels were written on papyrus, ancient writing material made from the pith of a reed that grows in the Nile Delta. The pith was flattened, and laid out on a flat surface, then more pith was added at a right angle, moistened, then pounded flat. The pith was then dried under pressure, and polished to make a sheet of writing material like paper from trees. In fact, the word *paper* is derived from the word *papyrus*. Papyrus was fragile unless kept in a dry climate, and documents written on papyrus had a relatively short shelf life, perhaps 100 years at most, which is one reason that animal skins ("parchment") were preferred over papyrus in moist climates such as Europe.

Scholars have confirmed that a papyrus fragment of the Gospel of John discovered in the early 20th century was copied as little as 30-40 years after the original writing. Catalogued as P[52] (signified by a Gothic "P" standing for a *papyrus* manuscript, and "52," the sequence of discovery among New Testament papyri), and called the John Rylands papyrus, P[52] is a business card-sized fragment of a portion of John chapter 18. It was identified in 1934 by C. H. Roberts and dated A.D. 125-130 (plus or minus 25 years) by textual critic Bart Ehrman.[12] P[52] has value in confirming the original wording of John's Gospel, but perhaps even greater value as evidence for a 1st century date for the original writing of the Gospel.

The discovery of P[52] destroyed the 19th century view of radical critic Ferdinand Christian Baur, who concluded, based on his assumption that John's Gospel contains "later Christological developments," that the Gospel attributed to John the Apostle must have been written by some unknown person around the year 170.[13]

How does the Manuscript Comparison Factor support the position that nothing in the text of the original Gospels has been lost?[14] Here is where the wealth of manuscript evidence for the New Testament books stands alone by comparison. If the texts of other works of classical antiquity are considered reliable despite several hundreds of years (and in most cases more than 1,000 years) between the original writing and the oldest copies, and since nearly all these ancient writings exist only in a handful of copies (not thousands, like the Gospels), then the reliability of the Gospels should not be questioned on textual grounds. Further, skeptics of the text of the Gospels should not be allowed a special pleading that holds the text of the Gospels to a different standard from all other works of antiquity. As Montgomery put it,

> To express skepticism of the resultant text of the New Testament books...is to allow all of classical antiquity to slip into obscurity, for no documents of the ancient period are as well attested bibliographically as the New Testament.[15]

## EVIDENCE THAT THE ORIGINAL TEXT OF THE GOSPELS CAN BE REASONABLY RECONSTRUCTED

The abundance of manuscripts attesting to the text of the Gospels is a two-edged sword. On the one hand, the manuscripts constitute hard evidence of the Gospels' textual tradition. On the other hand, more copies mean more variations. Indeed, copyists fell victim to the dictum *errare humanum est* ("to err is human"), not only copying the errors that were in their exemplar, but adding some of their own.

### HOW VARIATIONS IN THE TEXT AROSE

Until printing became available following Gutenberg's invention of moveable type, all documents were written and copied by hand. Most people know from experience that copying anything by hand almost inevitably leads to the copy's having variations from the original ("exemplar"). The lengthier the exemplar, the more changes are likely to creep in to the copy.

### THE NATURE OF VARIATIONS IN THE MANUSCRIPTS

The nature of variant readings in the Gospels and New Testament is often misunderstood, and skeptics often present the subject of variations in a way that leaves the impression it is impossible to make sense of the text. The evidence, however, does not support this unwarranted conclusion. The threshold consideration is, "what is a variation?"

"Variations" include such trivial things as spelling differences. For example, in Revelation 1:5 some manuscripts have the Greek word *lousanti_*("washed"), and others *lusanti_*("loosed, set free"). The words are pronounced the same, the difference being the addition of the "u" (upsilon) in the Greek word for "washed." Another common cause of variations is use of synonyms, such as substituting "Jesus" for "Lord," or vice versa, and the omission or inclusion of words (e.g., using "Jesus Christ" instead of "Lord Jesus Christ"). In rare instances, variations, involve the omission or inclusion of entire sentences. In short, every place manuscripts are not in agreement, no matter how trivial, counts as a variant reading, although most of these differences are minor and easy to resolve.

## UNINTENTIONAL ERRORS

By "errors" we mean any place where a copy deviates from the exemplar. There are unintentional errors and intentional errors. Unintentional copyist errors include misspelling words, using synonyms rather than the actual words found in the exemplar, and misreading the exemplar, resulting in leaving out or adding words. In addition, some copies of the Gospels were made in a *scriptorium,* whereby someone would slowly read from the exemplar, while several copyists wrote what they heard. This was an efficient way to create more than one copy at a time, but scriptoriums also fostered copyist errors due to faulty hearing. Because some words in Greek sound the same but are spelled differently and have different meanings (e.g., in English "there" and "their"), errors of hearing led to a number of variations in the manuscripts of the Gospels.

## INTENTIONAL ERRORS

Scribes sometimes intentionally changed the wording in their copies from the wording of the exemplar. In fact, in several manuscripts scribes went back and made "corrections" to the exemplar where the scribe believed there was an error. This sometimes led to later scribes' changing the exemplar back to the originally wording. Intentional changes included stylistic changes (e.g., modern differences between UK English "labour" and US English "labor"). Scribes also occasionally omitted material they thought was wrong, harsh or superfluous, and sometimes added material to explain a verse that the scribe was concerned could be misconstrued without inserting clarification.

## ILLUSTRATING HOW VARIATIONS BETWEEN COPIES CAN BE RESOLVED

Suppose you are sifting through several handwritten copies of a poem, and all of them except one begins "Mary had a little lamb." One copy reads, "Mary had a little lamp." Now, although it is possible that Mary had a little "lamp," since most people are familiar with the poem, and since all but one copy reads the way we heard the poem as children, it is obvious that "lamp" is not the correct word, but is a scribal error. Under these facts, the likely reason for the variation "lamp" is poor copying. This simply illustrates how textual criticism works—resolving variations that exist in copies of handwritten literature by using principles of textual analysis and common sense.

## THE NUMBER OF VARIATIONS IN NEW TESTAMENT MANUSCRIPTS-- TRIVIAL VERSUS SUBSTANTIAL

The next question is, "how many variations are there in the New Testament manuscripts?" Here is where critics often estimate but don't explain the number of variants. A case in point is Bart Ehrman's statement that there are more variants among the New Testament manuscripts than there are words in the New Testament. This could well be true given the vast number of Greek manuscripts, but the statement is essentially meaningless without any qualifiers, such as how many of these variants constitute "substantial variation." In fact, if we counted only "substantial variation" to give a realistic picture of the consistency of New Testament manuscripts, the amount would be minuscule.

The issue, for purposes of determining the reliability of the New Testament text, is not the *number* of variations, but the *significance* of variations.[16] If the amount of *significant* variations in the New Testament text is small, there is no reason to question the reliability of the New Testament, in general, or of the Gospels, specifically on textual grounds.

## THE SIGNIFICANCE OF VARIATIONS IN THE NEW TESTAMENT MANUSCRIPTS

In the year 1881, the patron saints of modern New Testament textual criticism, Brooke Foss Westcott and Fenton John Anthony Hort, wrote their seminal work, confidently titled *The New Testament in the Original Greek*. In addressing the significance of variations in the text, Westcott and Hort wrote:

> If comparative trivialities, such as changes of order, the insertion or omission of an article with proper names, and the like,

are set aside the words in our opinion still subject to doubt can hardly amount to more than a thousandth part of the whole New Testament.[17]

Textual critic Daniel B. Wallace agrees with the conclusion of Westcott and Hort, stating that "meaningful and viable" variations in the text involve "about 1 percent of all textual problems," and that "most New Testament scholars would say there are far fewer textual problems in this category than even 1 percent of the total."[18]

Even skeptical textual critic Bart Ehrman agrees that most variations among the New Testament manuscripts are trivial:

> Most of these differences are immaterial, insignificant, and important for nothing more than to show us that ancient scribes could spell no better than most people can today.[19]

Ehrman further acknowledges in the appendix of the paperback edition of *Misquoting Jesus,* "Essential Christian beliefs are not affected by textual variants in the manuscript tradition of the New Testament."[20]

Thus, the question of whether the text of the Gospels has been changed over the years is answered by the wealth of manuscript evidence and the application of textual criticism to the few meaningful and viable variations, resulting in the confident reconstruction of the original wording.

## CONCLUSION

Are the Gospels the same today as they were when originally written? Applying the Manuscript Comparison Factor, the results are clear: The Gospels and New Testament have better manuscript support than virtually all works of classic Graeco-Roman literature combined. If textual reliability is assumed for other ancient works, it cannot reasonably be doubted for the Gospels and the entire New Testament.

The manuscript comparison factor presents two indisputable facts: (1) No work of antiquity is anywhere near the Gospels in terms of how close in time the oldest manuscripts are to the original date of composition; and (2) no work of antiquity has anywhere near the number of extant manuscripts as the Gospels and the New Testament. Thus, unless the critic wants a special pleading that requires a different standard for New Testament documents as opposed to all other documents of antiquity, the critic must either dismiss all classical antiquity as textually unreliable, or else acknowledge that virtually the entire text of the New Testament is firmly established. The conclusion of apologist Ravi Zacharias makes the point:

> In real terms, the New Testament is easily the best attested ancient writing in terms of the sheer number of documents, the time span between the events and the document, and the variety of documents available to sustain or contradict it. There is nothing in ancient manuscript evidence to match such textual availability and integrity.[21]

Most textual critics acknowledge that the original text of the New Testament can reasonably be reconstructed from existing manuscripts, although some, like Ehrman, are reluctant to say we can "know" what the original said. Christian apologists should note that even scholars who are skeptical about the divinity or even the historicity of Jesus acknowledge a reliable New Testament textual tradition unparalleled in its manuscript support. These same scholars at times will echo the views of evangelical scholars on the issue of the significance of the variations in the text, concluding the variations affect no essential Christian doctrine.

Finally, few, if any, skeptics of Christianity reject the historicity or resurrection of Jesus because of textual problems. Most skeptics question the *historical* (not textual) reliability of the Gospel accounts, doubting whether they contain the actual words and deeds of Jesus of Nazareth. For skeptics with an *a priori* belief that there is no God, or who dismiss the possibility of miracles regardless of the evidence, nothing is likely to change their minds. But such a rigid adherence to naturalism or atheism means being philosophically close-minded. For skeptics willing to examine the evidence, an ancient text says, "Come now, let us reason together. Though your sins are as scarlet, they will be as white as snow; though they are red like crimson, they will be like wool" (Isaiah 1:18).

# CHAPTER SIX
# The Verdict from History and Archaeology

**Issue:** Do history and archaeology confirm the reliability of the Gospels?

**Argument:** History and archaeology confirm the reliability of the Gospel record

## EVIDENCE IN SUPPORT OF ARGUMENT

1. Historical investigation substantially confirms the historical statements in the Gospels.

2. Archaeology substantially confirms the people, places, names, titles and geography mentioned in the Gospels.

3. Archaeology now confirms many Gospel accounts that were previously questioned for lack of corroborating evidence.

4. The Gospel writers were the right people, in the right place, at the right time to accurately record the life and teachings of Jesus.

5. The conclusions of historical investigation of the Gospel accounts, together with evidence from archaeology, make a *prima facie* case for the Gospels' general reliability.

6. Early non-Christian sources, such as Josephus, Tacitus, Suetonius, Mara bar Serapion and Lucian of Samosata confirm many Gospel accounts.

7. Early Christian sources, including the New Testament Epistles, the *Didache*, Clement of Rome and Ignatius, confirm many Gospel accounts.

8. Experts in history and archaeology confirm the reliability of Gospel accounts.

9. The verified historical accuracy of the Gospels is evidence that the unverifiable claims in the Gospels can reasonably be accepted as true.

## GENERAL RELIABILITY OF THE GOSPELS

Thus far we have presented evidence that answers important questions about the historical reliability of the Gospels.

• Were the Gospels written when eyewitnesses to the life of Jesus were still alive? A resounding *Yes*.

• Were the people who wrote the Gospels truly the traditional authors Matthew, Mark, Luke, and John? Early evidence says *Yes*, plus there are no other names connected to the Gospels from any sources.

• Were the Gospel writers biased? *No*. The criterion of embarrassment, consistent with the evidentiary principle of "declaration against interest," is strong evidence that the Gospel writers told the truth, even when it was embarrassing to themselves, to the other disciples, and to Jesus.

• Were any authentic accounts of the life of Jesus kept out of the New Testament? *No*. The so-called "lost gospels" are spurious fabrications that add no verifiable facts to the ministry of Jesus.

• Can the original text of the Gospels be confidently determined from existing copies? *Yes*, owing to the wealth of evidence available for reconstructing the original wording.

The answers to the foregoing questions that relate to the reliability of the Gospels make a cumulative case for their general historical reliability. The evidence supports the conclusion that the writers were the right people, in the right place at the right time to accurately relay the life and teachings of Jesus. Their honest accounts, which have no rivals for information about the life and teachings of Jesus, have been copied extensively over the centuries, leaving a textual tradition that essentially contains the original wording.

With all these credentials of general reliability, one question remains regarding the Gospels' historical reliability: Do reliable sources outside of the Gospels substantiate their specific accounts? In short, when weighed in the balance of accepted history and archaeological findings, do the facts of history and findings of archaeology confirm what is found in the Gospel record?

## RELIABLE WHERE TESTABLE IS A SUBSTANTIAL REASON FOR ACCEPTING RELIABILITY WHERE NOT TESTABLE

Before addressing specific evidence for the historical reliability of the Gospels, a word about "spiritual claims" is appropriate. Some of the claims in the Gospels are subject to historical investigation, such as whether Jesus was crucified, and whether He appeared alive after His crucifixion. Some of the claims in the Gospels are not subject to historical investigation, a category we have labeled "spiritual claims."

We discussed the issue of "spiritual claims" previously, and made the point that there is no way to directly prove that a person's sins were forgiven despite Jesus saying so (cf. Matthew 9:2). The inability to directly prove spiritual claims is based on their intangible nature, that is, they are outside of the physical realm (i.e., "metaphysical") and cannot be verified by our senses.

As a way of circumstantially proving His spiritual authority, however, Jesus provided empirical evidence of His miraculous powers in the form of healing the paralytic. His healing miracle was tangible evidence that weighs heavily in favor of His untestable (i.e., "spiritual") claims being true. If Jesus conditioned His spiritual authority on healing a paralyzed man, it would seem to defy logic and take more faith for those present to reject His spiritual authority after the miracle had been performed.

A similar application of circumstantial evidence involves the historical event that is the foundation of Christianity, namely Jesus' resurrection from the dead. Although evidence can be adduced to support the historical claims that Jesus was crucified and later rose from the dead, no direct evidence can prove that the *source* of Jesus' resurrection was God Himself.

Direct evidence for the cause of the resurrection is beyond the scope of historical investigation, but we can certainly make a circumstantial case that the best explanation of the cause of Jesus' resurrection is that God raised Jesus. History can investigate the question of *whether* Jesus appeared alive after His crucifixion, whereas logic and reason make a circumstantial case for the *cause* of Jesus' resurrection. If the Gospel accounts of the resurrection are historically reliable, then it follows that the Gospel claims regarding the cause of Jesus being raised, namely God Himself, should be presumed reliable.

## PRESUMPTION OF RELIABILITY, OR PRESUMPTION OF UNRELIABILITY?

In the American justice system a person is innocent until proven guilty ("presumption of innocence"). Should the same presumption be applied to historical documents, that is, should they be considered reliable until proven unreliable? Going back as far as Aristotle, there is a principle that suggests a reader should look for ways to understand what a writer says in a way that does not assume contradictions and errors.[1]

Regardless of whether any historical document ought to be afforded the benefit of the doubt on the issue of reliability, the credentials of the Gospels thus far presented make a reasonable *prima facie* case for reliability. This turns the tables and puts the burden on the critic to produce equal or greater evidence of unreliability.

How have critics attempted to meet their burden? Primarily by arguing that certain references about people, places and customs in the Gospels are not supported by history and archaeology. Thus, the argument continues, if the Gospels are not reliable where they can be tested, i.e., references to people, places, events and customs, then they are surely not reliable where they cannot be tested, i.e., spiritual claims.

## SKEPTICS' ARGUMENTS FROM SILENCE DEFEATED BY ARCHAEOLOGICAL DISCOVERIES

Some critics contend that the lack of historical or archaeological confirmation of a Gospel reference is evidence the reference was fabricated. In response, fair-minded writers have pointed out that "absence of evidence is not evidence of absence." In other words, just because the Gospels make a reference to a person, place, event, custom, etc. that has not been confirmed by sources outside of the Gospels does not mean the unconfirmed reference is fiction.

A critic working 100 years ago could have compiled an extensive list of uncorroborated references in the Gospels. During the past 100 years that list would have shrunk considerably. Archaeology continues to uncover evidence that substantiates references in the Gospels that were previously unconfirmed and thus questioned. The following are a few recent examples of references in the Gospels that archaeology has confirmed, thereby adding weight to the argument that those Gospel accounts that remain unconfirmed should not be presumed unreliable:

## USE OF NAILS IN CRUCIFIXION

The Gospel accounts of Jesus' crucifixion do not specifically say He was nailed to a cross: Matthew 27:35: "When they had crucified Him...." Mark 15:24: "And they crucified Him." Luke 23:33: "And when they came to the place which is called The Skull, they crucified Him." John 19:18: "They crucified Him." Crucifixion was a Roman method of execution that was designed to inflict maximum suffering and humiliation. The condemned was stripped naked, affixed to an upright pole that usually included a crossbar, and then left out in the elements to die slowly. The body was typically left on the cross for several days to warn others of the consequences of defying Rome.

Although the Gospels do not say that Jesus was nailed to a cross, after His crucifixion Thomas tells the other disciples, "Unless I see the *nail* marks in his hands and put my finger where the *nails* were...I will not believe" (John 20:25). A week later Jesus appears and says to Thomas, "Put your finger here; see my hands" (John 20:27). Together these verses leave little doubt that John's Gospel affirms that nails were used in the crucifixion of Jesus. Also, in a post-resurrection appearance, when the disciples were wondering if it was truly Jesus, He tells them, "Look at my hands and my feet" (Luke 24:39). This is further evidence from Luke that Jesus' hands and feet bore the marks of crucifixion, which, presumably, meant nail prints.

Early 20th century critics seized on the Gospel references to nails and concluded that since no archaeological evidence had been uncovered showing 1st century Roman crucifixions used nails, the accounts must be a later tradition appended to the Gospels. This type of skepticism, essentially an argument from silence, was part of the cumulative case critics tried to make to question the reliability of the Gospels.

Those skeptical of the Gospel accounts that imply the use of nails for Jesus' crucifixion had trouble reconciling their skepticism with Roman historian Tacitus' account of Emperor Nero's brutality against Christians that occurred about A.D. 64. Tacitus writes that Nero, blaming Christians for the fire that burned much of Rome, inflicted tortures on them:

> Mockery of every sort was added to their deaths. Covered with the skins of beasts, they were torn by dogs and perished, or were nailed to crosses, or were doomed to the flames and burnt, to serve as a nightly illumination, when daylight had expired.[2]

Further, Jewish historian Flavius Josephus also acknowledge the Romans' use of nails for crucifixion, writing about A.D. 93 of the Jews' capture by the Romans during the Jewish War of A.D. 66-70:

> When caught, they resisted, and were then tortured and crucified before the walls as a terrible warning to the people within…Out of rage and hatred, the soldiers nailed their prisoners in different postures, so great was their number that space could not be found for their crosses.[3]

Critics had to walk back their skepticism over the nails issue when, in 1968, a box ("ossuary") containing the bones of one Yohannan ben Ha'galgol was excavated by archaeologist Vassilius Tzaferis in the East Jerusalem neighborhood of Giv'at ha-Mivtar. The remains have been dated to the period of around A.D. 70.[4] What was most revealing about Yohannan's remains was that a 4 ½ inch iron nail was protruding from one of his heel bones ("calcaneum"). The nail was bent, so it appeared that the difficulty of removing the metal nail for reuse was not worth the effort, and thus it was left protruding from the man's heel bone. It was clear that the man had been crucified, and a nail was used to affix his foot to a wooden cross. This finding was irrefutable evidence that metal nails were used in 1st century Roman crucifixions, a defeat for the critic who, up to 1968, used the lack of archaeological confirmation of metal nails in 1st century crucifixions to question the historical accuracy of the Gospels.

## PONTIUS PILATE

Pontius Pilate, the governor ("prefect") of Judea at the time of Jesus, plays a prominent role in the Gospel accounts of Jesus' trial and condemnation to crucifixion. Early 2nd century Roman historian Cornelius Tacitus (ca 110) refers to Jesus and Pilate, writing:

> Nero fastened the guilt and inflicted the most exquisite tortures on a class hated for their abominations, called Christians by the populace. Christus, from whom the name had its origin, suffered the extreme penalty during the reign of Tiberius at the hands of one of our procurators, Pontius Pilate.[5]

Prior to 1961 there was no physical evidence confirming the existence of Pontius Pilate. Critics even suspected the reference to Pilate in Tacitus was a "Christian interpolation" (i.e., added by some unknown

Christian to Tacitus' authentic writing). Then, in 1961, an inscription was found on a limestone block in Caesarea on the coast of modern Israel. The Latin inscription, now referred to as the "Pilate Stone," is damaged, but much of the inscription is intact. The original inscription likely read (translated into English):

To the Divine Augusti Tiberieum
Pontius Pilate
prefect of Judea
has dedicated this

The Pilate Stone confirms the existence of Pilate, previously known only from the Gospels, Josephus, and from later Roman histories that briefly mention Pilate. The artifact serves as further confirmation for the Gospel accounts being historical and not fictional.

## NAZARETH

Skeptics argued that the village of Nazareth, which all four canonical Gospels present as Jesus' hometown, did not exist in the 1st century A.D. because no evidence of Nazareth's existence during the time of Jesus had ever been found. The conclusion was that the Gospel writers had made up the references to Nazareth, which skeptics took as further evidence that Gospel accounts are not historically reliable.

The Gospels of Matthew and Luke state that Jesus grew up in a village called "Nazareth,"[6] and Jesus is referred to as "Jesus of Nazareth" 17 times in the New Testament. Apart from the Gospel references, early Christian writers Julius Africanus (ca 221) and Origen (ca 230) and Eusebius (ca 330) refer to Nazareth ("Nazara" or "Nazaret"). No non-Christian references to Nazareth existed until 1962, when an inscription referring to Nazareth was discovered on a piece of marble from a synagogue at Caesarea Maritima on the coast of modern Israel. The inscription dates to approximately A.D. 300.

The lack of Jewish references to Nazareth prior to A.D. 300, the lack of evidence from non-biblical 1st century sources, and the lack of archaeological evidence of a Jewish settlement at the time of Jesus caused skeptics to question whether Nazareth in the Gospels was a fiction. Then, in 2009, an Israeli archaeologist uncovered a house from the Jewish village of Nazareth claiming to date from the time of Jesus.[7] The discovery, if accurate, confirms the historicity of the Gospel references to Nazareth and defeats the skeptic's argument from silence that the Gospel accounts of Nazareth were fictitious.

## THE EXISTENCE OF JESUS

Despite a mountain of evidence, a few scholars take the fringe position that Jesus never lived.[8] One of the arguments these *mythicists* put forth is that there are several dozen writers who *should have* mentioned Jesus if He truly existed. As the theory goes, since Jesus is not mentioned by any of the writers who *should have* mentioned Him, Jesus must be a myth. This view was popularized by John Remsberg, who wrote a book in 1909 entitled *The Christ: A Critical Review and Analysis of the Evidence*[9] in which he provides a list of writers ("Remsberg's List") he contended should have referred to Jesus if Jesus was an historical person.

One ancient writer on Remsberg's List is Philo, a Jew from Alexandria, Egypt, some 300 miles from where Jesus lived. Remsberg erroneously says Philo lived "in or near Jerusalem," then rattles off a series of events at which he contends Philo was present, including when Jesus was born, made His triumphal entry into Jerusalem, was crucified, rose from the dead, and ascended into Heaven.[10] Remsberg makes Philo out to be the ancient equivalent of Forrest Gump,[11] the fictional movie character who was always in the right place at the right time to both observe and be a part of defining historic events. Using Remsberg's logic, the high priests of Judea during Philo's adult life must have never existed, because Philo never mentions them, either, despite their unique role in the life of the Jewish people.[12]

## NON-CHRISTIAN SOURCES CONFIRMING GOSPEL ACCOUNTS

Several early non-Christian sources confirm the historicity of Jesus and of other people and events recorded in the Gospels. Skeptics suggest that some of these sources are "Christian interpolations," namely glosses added to documents to support Christianity's teachings. Although a reference to Jesus by 1st century Jewish historian Flavius Josephus contains material the majority of scholars of all persuasions consider Christian interpolations, skeptics would like to "throw out the baby with the bathwater" by claiming that *all* early secular references to Jesus are suspect because they passed through Christian hands. This view is more fitting for the category of "pseudo-skepticism" than for genuine scholarly skepticism, for pseudo-skepticism is a category that includes those who will never accept an argument that favors the historical reliability of the Gospels, no matter how well evidenced. Despite a handful of mythicists who doubt whether Jesus ever existed, virtually all scholars, including atheists and agnostics, accept the fact that Jesus was an historical person who was crucified by the Romans. Several non-Christian sources confirm the existence of Jesus and aspects of the Gospel accounts. In addition, there are many early Christian writers similarly, but in much more detail, corroborate the content of the Gospels.

## FLAVIUS JOSEPHUS

Josephus was born A.D. 37, and around the year 93 wrote over 20 volumes on the history of the Jewish people called *Antiquities of the Jews.* In *Antiquities* Josephus makes two references to Jesus--in book 18.3.3 and in book 20.9.1. The references to Jesus have provoked a significant amount of discussion as to their authenticity. Passage 18.3.3 reads as follows:

> Now there was about this time Jesus, a wise man, if it be lawful to call him a man, for he was a doer of wonderful works, a teacher of such men as receive the truth with pleasure. He drew over to him both many of the Jews, and many of the Gentiles. He was the Christ; and when Pilate, at the suggestion of the principal men amongst us, had condemned him to the cross, those that loved him at the first did not forsake him, for he appeared to them alive again the third day, as the divine prophets had foretold these and ten thousand other wonderful things concerning him; and the tribe of Christians, so named from him, are not extinct to this day.

The passage is called the *Testimonim Flavianum* ("testimony of Flavius [Josephus]), and is cited by Church historian Eusebius (ca 350). Eusebius' version is almost unanimously considered to contain "interpolations" added to an authentic core.[13] Thus, the passage is often cited with brackets identifying the presumed interpolations as follows:

> Now there was about this time Jesus, a wise man, [if it be lawful to call him a man,] for he was a doer of wonderful works,

a teacher of such men as receive the truth with pleasure. He drew over to him both many of the Jews, and many of the Gentiles. [He was the Christ;] and when Pilate, at the suggestion of the principal men amongst us, had condemned him to the cross, those that loved him at the first did not forsake him, [for he appeared to them alive again the third day, as the divine prophets had foretold these and ten thousand other wonderful things concerning him;] and the tribe of Christians, so named from him, are not extinct to this day.

Most scholars accept the non-bracketed part of the *Testimonim Flavianum* as authentic.[14] As such, it is the earliest corroboration of the historical Jesus outside of the New Testament. An Arabic version of the passage, although much later (10th century) than the Eusebius version (ca 350), does not contain most of the problematic wording that scholars typically reject as interpolations. The Arabic version of the passage, reads as follows:

"At this time there was a wise man who was called Jesus. And His conduct was good, and known to be virtuous. And many people from among the Jews and other nations became his disciples. Pilate condemned Him to be crucified and die. And those who had become his disciples did not abandon his discipleship. They reported that He had appeared to them three days after his crucifixion and that He was alive; accordingly, He was perhaps the Messiah concerning whom the prophets have recounted wonders."

In the second reference to Jesus in *Antiquities*, found in 20.9.1, Josephus refers to Jesus as "the so-called Christ." The passage deals with the death of the procurator Festus (see Acts 24:27-26:32) whom Caesar replaced with Albinus, and recounts the leading Jews' concern that the High Priest Ananus, son of Ananus ("Annas" mentioned in the Gospels and Acts) had not waited for approval from Albinus before assembling the Sanhedrin,[15] who proceeded to condemn James, the brother of Jesus, and others to death:

Festus was now dead, and Albinus was but upon the road; so he assembled the Sanhedrin of judges, and brought before them the brother of Jesus, who was called Christ, whose name was James, and some others; and when he had formed an accusation against them as breakers of the law, he delivered them to be stoned: but as for those who seemed the most equitable of the citizens, and such as were the most uneasy at the breach of the laws, they disliked what was done; they also sent to the king, desiring him to send to Ananus that he should act so no more, for that what he had already done was not to be justified; nay, some of them went also to meet Albinus, as he was upon his journey from Alexandria, and informed him that it was not lawful for Ananus to assemble a Sanhedrin without his consent.

Regarding Josephus' second reference to Jesus, pre-eminent Josephus scholar Louis Feldman writes: Almost all scholars have accepted as authentic Josephus' reference (Ant. 20.200) to James, "the brother of Jesus who was called the Christ."[16] Feldman's conclusion is echoed by New Testament scholar Richard Bauckham, "the vast majority of scholars have considered it to be authentic."[17]

Josephus also mentions John the Baptist (*Antiquities* 20.9.1). These references to Jesus and John the Baptist in *Antiquities* provide evidence from outside the Gospels that confirm the existence of people and events mentioned in the Gospels. This historical corroboration provides the type of cumulative evidence that entitles the Gospels to a presumption of historical reliability. New Testament scholar James Charlesworth agrees: "We can now be as certain as historical research will presently allow that Josephus did refer to Jesus," thereby providing "corroboration of the gospel account."[18]

## CORNELIUS TACITUS

Tacitus was a Roman historian and senator. He is regarded as the greatest historian of the Roman Empire.[19] About A.D. 115 Tacitus wrote a 16-volume work called *Annals*, about half of which survive. In *Annals,* volume 15, he described events during the reign of Emperor Nero, which began about 25 years after the time of Jesus. In that volume, Tacitus refers to the death of Christ and the existence of Christians in Rome:

> [Nero]. . . to suppress the rumor [that he had ordered the burning of Rome] falsely charged with the guilt, and punished with the most exquisite tortures, the persons commonly called Christians, who were hated for their enormities. Christus, the

founder of the name, was put to death by Pontius Pilate, procurator of Judea in the reign of Tiberius . . . *Annals*, 15.44.

Tacitus was hardly a sympathetic witness to Christianity, and skeptics of Christianity cannot find a foothold in Tacitus' statement about Jesus to justify claiming it is a later Christian interpolation. So, what does the skeptic say to marginalize the historic value of Tacitus' reference to Jesus? Some argue that Tacitus got the information from an unreliable source, possibly Christians, and is merely passing along unconfirmed hearsay.[20] This argument falls under its own weight when we discover that Tacitus himself warned strongly against the use of hearsay.[21] Further, when he was not certain of the accounts he documented, Tacitus used qualifiers such as "according to some" and "the common account is."[22] Note that he used no qualifiers when referring to Jesus.

Tacitus, then, is the earliest Roman historian to refer to Jesus, confirming several details mentioned in the Gospels, including Pilate, and used the term "Christians" for followers of Jesus and cited Jesus' execution under Pilate during the reign of Tiberius.

## SUETONIUS

Gaius Suetonius Tranquillus was a Roman historian and a court official under Emperor Hadrian. He wrote biographies of 12 successive Roman Emperors, from Julius Caesar to Domitian, called *The Lives of Caesar*. Writing about the year A.D. 120, Suetonius mentioned Christ: "As the Jews were making constant disturbances at the instigation of Chrestus he expelled them from Rome." *Life of Claudius*, 25.4.

"Chrestus" is understood as an alternate spelling for *Christus*, the Latin form of the word for *Christ*. Suetonius also wrote, "Punishment by Nero was inflicted on the Christians, a class of men given to a new and mischievous superstition." *Life of Nero*, 16.2.

## PLINY THE YOUNGER

Pliny was the governor of Bithynia in Asia Minor (modern Turkey) and a friend of Roman author Suetonius. His uncle, Pliny the Elder, was a prominent Roman author and commander. Pliny the Younger in about A.D. 112 wrote a letter to the Roman Emperor Trajan, seeking counsel on how to treat Christians. Pliny had been severely punishing them for failing to recognize the Roman Emperor as divine, going as far as killing men and women, and even boys and girls who would not curse Christ and bow in worship to the Emperor. So many were being put to death that Pliny wondered if he should continue killing everyone who was discovered to be a Christian, or if he should kill only certain ones. In referring to the Christians, Pliny writes, in *Epistles* 10:96,

> They affirmed, however, that the whole of their guilt, or their error, was, that they were in the habit of meeting on a certain fixed day before it was light, when they sang in alternate verse a hymn to Christ as to a god, and bound themselves to a solemn oath, not to any wicked deeds, but never to commit any fraud, theft, adultery, never to falsify their word....

Pliny's letter corroborates, in the generation after the Apostles, that Jesus was worshipped as God, and that His followers were practicing the teachings of Jesus found in the Gospels. Pliny's letter is further corroboration from outside the Gospels and the New Testament that Jesus was revered as an historical person consistent with the life and teachings of Jesus presented in the Gospels.

## MARA BAR SERAPION

Mara bar Serapion was a Syrian philosopher who wrote a letter to his son, Serapion, likely between A.D. 73-100.[23] The letter, which is preserved in the British Museum in a 6th century manuscript, says: "What advantage did the Jews gain from executing their wise King?... Nor did the wise King die for good; he lived on in the teaching which He had been given."

Some scholars see Mara bar Serapion's letter as the earliest non-Christian reference to the crucifixion of Jesus.[24]

## LUCIAN OF SAMOSATA

Lucian was a satirist who wrote around the middle of the 2nd century (ca 170). Little is known about his life, but he was a prolific writer to whom dozens of surviving works are attributed. In *The Passing of Peregrinus* Lucian refers to Christ as "...the man who was crucified in Palestine because he introduced this new cult into the world..." Lucian referred to Christians as "worshipping that crucified sophist himself and living under his laws." Lucian is another example of a non-Christian writer who within 150 years of the time of Jesus referred to Jesus as an historical person consistent with what we find in the Gospels.

## THALLUS

Thallus was a Roman historian whose wrote several volumes around the year A.D. 50. His works are not extant except for a few fragments and quotations cited in Julius Africanus in his *History of the World* (ca 220), a work that is also not extant. However, an 8th century writer, Georgius Syncellus, cites a passage from *History of the World* in which Africanus takes Thallus to task for trying to explain away the darkness at Jesus' crucifixion as a natural phenomenon (i.e., a solar eclipse). According to Syncellus, Africanus writes: "Thallus, in the third book of his histories, explains away this darkness as an eclipse of the sun—unreasonably, as it seems to me."

If, indeed, Thallus was aware of the darkness at Jesus' crucifixion, his attempt to explain it away, as indicated by Julius Africanus and cited by Georgius Syncellus, is the earliest non-Christian reference to the crucifixion. However, there are many plausible alternative explanations to what Syncellus cites, so we should give it the appropriate weight as a possible early confirmation of events recorded in the Gospels.

## CHRISTIAN SOURCES CONFIRMING GOSPEL ACCOUNTS

Several early Christian writings confirm accounts from the Gospels, including one of the New Testament Epistles quoting a canonical Gospel and calling it "Scripture." These sources add further historical confirmation to the general reliability of Gospel accounts.

## PAUL'S LETTER TO TIMOTHY

In 1 Timothy 5:18 Paul begins by saying, "For the Scripture says," then writes, "The laborer is worthy of his wages." The Greek text of this last phrase is word for word the same as Luke 10:7.[25] Paul's apparent quotation from the Gospel of Luke is evidence that Paul knew of the Gospel of Luke and believed that Luke was reliable and accurate in quoting Jesus and that his Gospel belonged to the category of "Scripture."[26]

## CLEMENT OF ROME

Writing about A.D. 95, Clement makes references to the "Gospel" and quotes from Matthew, Mark and Luke, referring to them as the words of Jesus.[27]

*Didache*

The *Didache* ("teaching of the 12") was written about A.D. 95 and refers to the Gospels twice and cites portions found in Matthew, Mark and Luke.

## IGNATIUS OF ANTIOCH

Writing about A.D. 115, Ignatius, Bishop of Antioch, refers to words of Jesus found in Luke.[28]

## POLYCARP

Writing about A.D. 115, Polycarp cites words of Jesus found in Matthew chapters 5, 6, 7 and 26.[29]

## CALLING IN THE EXPERTS

In the quest to find out whether the Gospel record is consistent with the conclusions of history and archaeology, it is important to consult the experts in those fields. Before presenting the opinions of experts, it is necessary to understand the role of experts so that the opinions they render are given the appropriate weight. In courts of law, lawyers will often engage the services of expert witnesses to testify about a fact in dispute.

Federal Rule of Evidence 702 sets forth the parameters of expert witness testimony:

A witness who is qualified as an expert by knowledge, skill, experience, training, or education may testify in the form of an opinion or otherwise if:

(a) the expert's scientific, technical, or other specialized knowledge will help the trier of fact to understand the evidence or to determine a fact in issue;

(b) the testimony is based on sufficient facts or data;

(c) the testimony is the product of reliable principles and methods; and

**(d)** the expert has reliably applied the principles and methods to the facts of the case.

Before testifying, an expert witness's credentials are presented in open court, and the opposing side can challenge the expert's qualifications to testify on a fact in dispute. Once the witness is qualified to the court's satisfaction, the expert may testify within the witness's area of special knowledge, and can render an opinion.

For example, I tried a case in which my client, while driving on the freeway, sustained a severe back injury when another vehicle struck his vehicle from behind. One issue was how fast the vehicle that struck my client's car was traveling at impact. I engaged an engineer whose expertise was in accident reconstruction. One of the undisputed facts was that the impact caused my client's seat to break loose.

My expert testified that the automaker of my client's vehicle had engineering specs that calculated how much force was necessary for the driver's seat to break loose. Based on those specs and other factors of physics, I asked the expert his opinion of the speed at impact, and he testified a "minimum of 40 miles per hour." An expert's opinion does not constitute an incontrovertible fact, and the opposition is free to call its own expert. The fact that a witness is qualified as an expert means the person has earned the right to have his or her opinion heard.

## WHEN EXPERTS DO NOT AGREE

As a trial lawyer, I have been involved in many trials where the expert witness for each side gave opinions about facts in dispute that were diametrically opposite--what lawyers and judges call "dueling experts." A jury must then listen and decide which expert was more credible. Quite often judges will say, privately, that most dueling experts "cancel each other out," meaning no clear "winner" emerges from their conflicting testimony. There are exceptions. For example, consider the facts of the injury case referred to earlier.

Before the accident my client, who was about 30 years old, was healthy and pain-free. Immediately following the accident he experienced severe back pain, and was still in pain more than a year later when the trial occurred. During treatment for his pain, it was discovered that my client had a pre-existing condition in his spine that he was unaware of,[30] a condition that many people suffer without experiencing pain.[31] At trial, the defense retained an orthopedic surgeon with 45 years of experience to testify as an expert about my client's injuries. The defense expert testified that the pre-existing condition in my client's spine was the cause of the severe pain my client had suffered for over a year. My cross-examination went something like this:

> JS: "Dr., it is your testimony that the severe pain (my client) has been in for more than a year is solely due to his pre-existing spinal condition?"
> Dr.: "Yes."
> JS: "And you admit that my client has had his spinal condition for 15 or more years?"
> Dr.: "Yes."
> JS: "And you heard (my client) testify that he had no back pain until immediately following the accident?"
> Dr.: "Yes."
> JS: "And it is your testimony that the pain (my client) has experienced following the accident is unrelated to the accident?"
> Dr.: "Yes."
> JS: "Let me see if I have this straight. It is your testimony that (my client) had a pre-existing condition in his spine for more than 15 years that had never caused him pain, then immediately after his car was struck from behind at a speed of over 40 miles per hour, with sufficient impact that the seat of his car broke loose, just coincidentally, unrelated to the accident, his pre-existing spinal condition chose that moment to start causing pain?"
> Dr.: "Yes."
> JS: "No further questions."

Unsurprisingly, the jury did not buy the physician's testimony regardless of his years of experience and impeccable credentials. The jury recognized the expert was trying to support a position that defied common sense.

When it comes to experts, it is important to consider not only credentials but also signs of objectivity and reason in their conclusions. If conclusions are based on sufficient evidence, they should be given proper weight. But positions based on "reading between the lines" or that otherwise involve speculation rather than an appeal to facts should be avoided. Still, honest scholars can look at the same data and come to different conclusions, and for a multitude of reasons. Even within the Gospels we find people who were presented with overwhelming evidence and yet chose to accept neither the evidence nor the claims connected to the evidence.[32]

## TESTIMONY FROM EXPERTS

As we can see from the back-injury case, it is human nature to embrace experts whose opinions align with our own. What is a layperson to think when competent scholars cannot agree on important issues? A few observations are in order. First, when people with academic credentials offer an opinion, it is worthy of consideration even if the opinion does not reflect the current "mainstream" of scholarship. Scholarly consensus can be wrong, but dismissing it lightly or solely because it challenges the truth of one's own thinking shows a reluctance to "go wherever the evidence leads."

"Thinking outside the box," however, and going against the consensus worked out well for forward thinkers such as Albert Einstein. If a qualified scholar holds an opinion that is not shared by most scholars in the field, rather than rejecting the opinion out of hand, we should find out how the scholar arrived at the opinion. Second, we should try to determine if any biases color the opinion. For example, those who do not believe that miracles are possible will not be convinced by all the evidence in the world that Jesus rose from the dead.

Philosopher C. Stephen Evans addresses the issue of whether a layperson ought to defer to scholarly consensus on issues such as the historical reliability of the Gospel of John. Evans writes:

> ...a person does not have to form and hold beliefs about John on the basis of critical scholarship in order to have beliefs that are reasonable.... I do not think that a layperson must on this question defer to expert opinion.[33]

Evans adds that it is erroneous for a non-philosopher to conclude that a certain philosophical view must be accepted because most philosophers hold it. In fact, accepting something solely because the majority does is a logical fallacy know as *argumentum ad populum* ("appeal to the people").

With respect to the issue of whether lay people ought to follow the scholarly consensus, Evans writes,

> ...someone who is not a biblical scholar is not rationally obligated to regard John as historically suspect just because this is the view of a majority of scholars at a particular time. The intelligent layperson will in any case recognize that such facts can change, and that scholarly disciplines are subject to fads and tendencies in much the same way as other groups of humans.[34]

## CONCLUSION ON THE GOSPELS' RELIABILITY FROM HISTORY AND ARCHAEOLOGY

Historian John Warwick Montgomery asks, "What, then, does a historian know about Jesus Christ? He knows, first and foremost, that the New Testament documents can be relied upon to give an accurate portrait of Him."[35] Critical New Testament scholar A. M. Hunter agrees, even though he does not believe the Gospel writers were eyewitnesses, and sets forth four reasons why the Gospels are reliable:

1. The early Christians were meticulous in preserving the tradition of Jesus' words and life.
2. The Gospel writers were close to the eyewitnesses and pursued the facts about Jesus.
3. There are indications that these authors were honest reporters.
4. The overall composite of Jesus as presented in the four Gospels is essentially the same.[36]

The Encyclopedia Britannica addresses the evidence from early non-Christian sources regarding the historicity of Jesus, stating

> These independent accounts prove that in ancient times even the opponents of Christianity never doubted the historical accuracy of Jesus, which was disputed for the first time and on inadequate grounds by several authors at the end of the 18th, during the 19th, and at the beginning of the 20th centuries.[37]

Historians Gary Habermas and Michael Licona find 42 references, in both Christian and non-Christian sources and from within

150 years of the time of Jesus, that confirm the historicity of Jesus.[38] There is abundant evidence corroborating the Gospel accounts of the life and teachings of Jesus, and even skeptic Bart Ehrman agrees when he discusses Luke's Gospel:

> There may indeed be fictional elements in the account, as we will see; but judging from the preface to volume one [i.e., Luke's gospel], from the subject matter of the narrate (the spread of the Christian church) and from the main characters themselves (who are, after all, historical persons), we can more plausibly conclude that Luke meant to write a history of early Christianity, not a novel. Moreover, all of the ancient Christian authors who refer to the book appear to have understood it in this way.[39]

New Testament scholar Craig L. Blomberg, whose detailed treatise on the reliability of the Gospels merits consideration from believers and skeptics alike, concludes his discussion with this statement:

> Whether by giving the Gospels the benefit of the doubt that all narratives of purportedly historical events merit or by approaching them with an initial suspicion in which every detail must satisfy the criteria of authenticity, the Gospels may be accepted as trustworthy accounts of what Jesus said and did. One cannot hope to prove the accuracy of every detail on purely historical grounds alone; there is simply not enough data available for that. But we may certainly speak of "general reliability."[40]

Indeed, Montgomery, Hunter, Habermas, Licona, Ehrman, Blomberg and a host of other historians and New Testament scholars confirm that the Gospels claim to be historical accounts, were written as historical accounts ("ancient biographies") and essentially prove to be historical accounts based on all available evidence. Therefore, a seeker of truth should read the Gospels and find out firsthand why the Galilean carpenter has had the greatest impact on history than any other person, and why He is worshipped as Lord by billions of people today.

# CHAPTER SEVEN
# Conclusion

I once had a court case in which the judge made an adverse ruling that prevented my client's case from advancing. The ruling was not supported by the facts of the case or the law. In a motion for reconsideration (a narrow remedy that affords parties an opportunity to revisit a court ruling) I prepared a list of 12 points designed to persuade the judge to change his ruling and let my client's case proceed.

After hearing the first three of my points, before I got to the fourth point, the judge said, "My previous ruling is vacated. The court rules that the case can now move forward." The judge had been convinced, based on evidence and reason, that my argument was solid. He had heard enough to change his mind. Some judges in this situation might have needed to hear six of the points, or even all 12, before granting my request. From my experience, it is also possible that some judges might not have agreed with my arguments despite the strong evidence in support.

There is a parallel from the above-cited case to the question of the reliability of the Gospels as a source of accurate information about the life and teachings of Jesus. Some people will conclude that the Gospels are true based on faith or tradition. Others may trust the Gospels based on one or two established facts. Still others may need all available evidence before accepting the general reliability of the Gospels. The preceding six chapters have made a substantial case for the reliability of the Gospels regardless of how much evidence a person requires before concluding the Gospel accounts are true.

## GOSPELS WERE WRITTEN CLOSE ENOUGH TO THE EVENTS TO BE CONSIDERED RELIABLE

Chapter One puts to rest the skeptic's claim that the Gospels could not have been written by eyewitnesses or those connected to eye witnesses. Even if one concedes, for the sake of argument, that the dates the Gospels were written at the latest possible dates scholars assign, eyewitness accounts are not precluded. Evidence has been provided from credible historical sources that the Apostle John, Son of Zebedee, lived until after the turn of the century. Thus, even an A.D. 100 date for John's Gospel does not eliminate John as a candidate for authorship of the Fourth Gospel. The same is true if late dates are assigned to Matthew, Mark, and Luke.

Additionally, the consensus of scholarship today accepts the probability that there was a written source for the life and teachings of Jesus that predates the canonical Gospels ("Q" for *quelle*, the German word for "source"). According to this popular view, Matthew, Mark and Luke relied on this proto-gospel material to some degree, which means the material found in the canonical Gospels that may have come from Q is early, i.e., close to the time of Jesus.

Finally, the events presented in the Gospels are the type that is easily remembered due to their unique and emotional status. Regardless of whether the writings were one decade or six decades removed from the events, some things we observe stay vividly in our memories our entire lives. This most certainly is true for those who saw the miracles of Jesus and heard His teachings firsthand. The recollections of eyewitnesses, as written themselves or told others, make a compelling case regardless of how long it took to reduce the recollections to writing.

## IDENTITY OF THE GOSPEL WRITERS

In responding to the purveyors of the "anonymous Gospels" argument, a well-known statement by the second President of the United States, John Adams, is apt: "Facts are stubborn things; and whatever may be our wishes, our inclinations, or the dictates of our passion, they cannot alter the state of facts and evidence."

It is undisputed that *no* historical statements or traditions exist that mention anyone other than Matthew, Mark, Luke and John being the authors of the canonical Gospels. It is also undisputed that *every* extant manuscript of the Gospels that contains the beginning portion lists Matthew, Mark, Luke or John as the writer. In the same way that Roman historian Tacitus does not identify himself within his writings as the author of his works, so also the Gospels within their texts do not specifically identify the writers.

Some of the Gospels, however, contain strong clues within as to who wrote them. For example, Luke's Gospel is part one of a two-part treatise dedicated to Theophilus, and the identity of the writer of Acts is almost certainly the writer of the Gospel of Luke. Since Luke is essentially the only candidate for authorship of Acts, then the only reasonable conclusion is that Luke, the beloved physician, wrote the Gospel of Luke. John's Gospel makes statements that claim the writer was an eyewitness of the events. Identifying John, the Son of Zebedee as the "disciple whom Jesus loved," and also as the author of the Fourth Gospel, makes logical sense, in the same way that no one disputes Tacitus' authorship, given the evidence from history and internal evidence.

Those who remain unconvinced after considering all the well-established evidence for the traditional authorship of the Gospels should keep in mind that the identity of the authors, despite being well established by the evidence, is not crucial to the issue of the Gospels' reliability. Unknown authors, and even pseudonymous writers can still provide reliable history. Because external sources confirm much of the core of the accounts in the Gospels that are subject to verification, the Gospels' reliability stands despite who wrote them.

## BIAS

When a judge considers testimony and renders a decision, the ruling is based on deliberation and a weighing of the evidence. Consider a case in which the judge presides over a criminal trial, not having any prior knowledge of what truly happened. If the judge rules the defendant ("accused") is guilty of the charged offense, and later writes a book about the trial, it would make no sense to conclude that the book is unreliable because the judge was biased for having found the defendant guilty. The judge's opinion was shaped by the evidence, not by bias, so the judge's ruling does not logically negate the reliability of his writing.

When we apply this reasoning to the Gospels, we acknowledge that the writers were convinced, *based on evidence*, that Jesus was the Messiah. To reach any other conclusion is to disregard the unique and miraculous works and teachings of Jesus as being the reason the writers believed in Jesus as Messiah.

Beyond the obvious reasons for presenting reliable accounts of Jesus, namely that they (or others they knew) were eyewitnesses to

Jesus' life, there are more subtle reasons to deem the Gospel accounts reliable. If the writers were trying to convince readers that the story of Jesus and His followers is one of flawless perfection, they failed miserably. The Gospels contain express and implied accusations against Jesu--that He was an illegitimate child, demon-possessed, mentally unstable, a drunkard, and many other defamatory statements. Gospel accounts also include Jesus' physical limitations such as being tired and hungry, and knowledge limitations, such as not knowing when He is returning to earth, or, in one instance, who touched His garment.

The disciples are exposed as fearful, faithless, wavering, dense and confused. Jesus calls Simon Peter, one of His "inner three" disciples, "Satan." One would not expect to find such details if the accounts are fictional. Instead, a fictional account would not have three women and only one man (John) at the cross of Jesus. A contrived account would have the disciples at the cross, standing bravely against the Romans instead of hiding in fear.

The criterion of embarrassment, including embarrassing details that put the main characters in a negative light, is an accepted criterion that supports a writer's being objective and unbiased. Those who might dispute the criterion of embarrassment as a reason to accept the reliability of the Gospel accounts must explain why such embarrassing detail is included, since these details do not advance the main theme of presenting Jesus as the Messiah.

## "LOST GOSPELS"

Many people find conspiracy theories entertaining, but most such theories rely on innuendos and suppositions that are based on meager facts stretched to the breaking point. The so-called "lost gospels" are equivalent to conspiracy theories in that one must assume, without any evidence, that the lost gospels contain suppressed truth about Jesus, and that we can know more today than those living in the 1st and 2nd centuries.

Chapter Four makes the point that the term "lost gospels" is a misnomer, since these documents were not *lost* and are not *gospels*. Instead, the common elements of these non-canonical writings is that they are forgeries, that is, they falsely attribute authorship to a known person who appears in true Gospel accounts. Additionally, since the life of Jesus during his three-year ministry is well-established in the canonical

Gospels, the "lost gospels" often adorn their writings with stories of Jesus as an infant or toddler. Some include "secret" conversations Jesus had with such figures as Mary Magdalene, Thomas, and even Judas Iscariot. This "secret," esoteric content in many of the "lost gospels" is quite the give-away as to the actual source, since the fingerprints of Gnosticism are all over theses writings.

As when parents find a piece of chocolate cake is missing, and then see their toddler with chocolate frosting on face and hands, it does not take Sherlock Holmes to figure out *whodunit*. The 2nd century heresy of Gnosticism is responsible for many of the spurious accounts of Jesus' life, stories created to align Jesus with the ethereal beliefs of Gnostics. In addition, some of the "lost gospels" appear to be attempts at pious fiction, providing Christians with an alternative to immoral novels that were available in the early centuries.

The fatal blow to the supposition that the "lost gospels" contain reliable information about Jesus not found in the Gospels is their late date. Most scholars would agree that the "lost gospels" are no earlier than the mid-to-late 2nd century, meaning the earliest they were written is 120-150 years after the time of Jesus. Many of these "lost gospels" are from 200-300 years after Jesus, hardly a time when new knowledge of Jesus could reliably be ascertained. Scholars agree that the "lost gospels" provide no new, verifiable information about the life of Jesus. The best and nearly exclusive source of reliable information about Jesus is found in the canonical Gospels of Matthew, Mark, Luke, and John.

## CHANGED OVER THE YEARS, OR NOT?

When addressing the issue of whether our existing New Testament text accurately reflects what was originally written in the 1st century, two important points weigh in:

(1) We do not possess any of the original writings (autographs).
(2) The copies we possess have variations in the text.

Textual criticism is the art and science of determining the original wording of any literature where the original is unknown (i.e., lost, destroyed, missing). Textual criticism examines the handwritten copies ("manuscripts") and uses accepted principles to filter out variations in the text and thus arrive at what was likely the original wording.

Textual criticism must be applied to virtually all documents from antiquity, including writings as recent as the works of Shakespeare (d. about 1610). One way to determine whether the original text of literature can be reliably reconstructed is to ask what textual evidence exists for making the determination. Evidence includes manuscripts in the receptor language, translations ("versions") of the literature, and any quotations of the literature outside of the work being examined.

Few, if any, works of antiquity are considered unreliable merely because scant textual evidence is available to confirm the original wording. Since this is the case, it is only fair not to disparage the text of the Gospels if they enjoy the same or better textual evidence than literature whose text is never questioned.

So, how does the text of the Gospels compare to other ancient documents? Chapter Five discusses the "Manuscript Comparison Factor," that analyzes (1) how close to the original writing are our oldest copies, and (2) how many copies exist? The smaller the gap between the autographs and the oldest copies, the more textually reliable the literature, since there were likely fewer generations of copying of the text, and since copying is what produces variations. The more manuscripts that exist of the literature, the better a textual tradition can be established. Using these criteria, how do the Gospels compare with other literature? The text of the Gospels—and in fact the text of the entire New Testament--is more reliable than any 10 pieces of literature of antiquity combined! Having a reliable text does not make the contents true, since we may possess a reliable text of fictional works such as the *Iliad*, but the embarrassing wealth of textual evidence does defeat the argument that the Gospels have been changed over the years.

## HISTORY AND ARCHAEOLOGY

Many, if not most, historical and archaeological references in the Gospels have been confirmed to some degree. Through the mid-20th century skeptics questioned the accuracy of Gospel references to people, places, events and customs that had not been corroborated by history or archaeology. No benefit of the doubt was given to the Gospels, and the lack of corroboration was take as evidence of inaccuracy, embellishment, or outright fiction. After the birth of modern Israel in 1948, archaeology in Israel experienced a resurgence, and many of the previously unconfirmed references in the Gospels have been confirmed, such as the use of nails in 1st century Roman crucifixions, the existence of Pontius Pilate and the existence of a village in 1st century A.D. Nazareth. Some skeptics have the temerity to argue that Jesus never existed. It would be unprecedented in history for a non-existent person to have the impact on humanity that Jesus has had. Because of the multiple sources within 100 years of Jesus that confirm His existence, the mythicist view deserves to be relegated to the fringe. The confirmation of the historical Jesus by Roman historian Tacitus and Jewish chronicler Flavius Josephus are, by themselves, sufficient to bury the mythicist position.

Even skeptic Bart Ehrman confirms the fact that the Gospels attempt to be a history of early Christianity, specifically in the case of the Gospel of Luke. The fact that Gospel writers such as John have an evangelistic purpose in mind does not negate the accuracy of what they present. The genre of the Gospels is that of ancient biographies. This approach includes such literary conventions as paraphrasing speeches, using a composite character to communicate facts that historically came from more than one source, approximation in numbers, and not being concerned with strict accuracy on peripheral details. The main topics, despite the flexibility in presenting peripheral details, are not called into question because of inexactness of the minutia. Whether there was one angel or two at the tomb of Jesus, or whether Jesus exorcised one or two demon-possessed men, do not weigh on the question of whether Jesus lived, died by crucifixion, and rose from the dead.

## WHAT IF I STILL CAN'T TRUST THE GOSPELS AS RELIABLE LITERATURE FOR THE LIFE AND TEACHINGS OF JESUS?

As one who engages in Christian Apologetics (i.e., giving evidence and reasons why Christianity is true), I run across people who, despite the evidence, still do not trust the Gospels as being reliable literature. I never concede the point of the Gospels not being reliable, since the cumulative evidence makes such a substantial case in their favor. I do, however, entertain the hypothetical, "What if the Gospels are not sufficiently historically reliable? Does your trust in Jesus depend on the Gospels being accurate?" My answer is, "No."

This may sound counter-intuitive, since I spend the first six chapters of this book making an evidential case for the Gospels. Am I saying that, despite the contrary evidence, I will continue to believe in Jesus? No, that would be "fideism," i.e., reliance on faith alone, to the point of rejecting reason, to obtain religious truth. So, how can I affirm the crucifixion and resurrection of Jesus without the Gospels? The simple answer is: The Epistles.

Many Christian Apologists (e.g., Gary Habermas, the leading evangelical scholar on the resurrection) conclude that the best evidence for the resurrection of Jesus is found in Paul's letters, especially 1 Corinthians and Galatians. How can this be? Because these letters give us a time line back to the event of the resurrection that even agnostic scholars such as Bart Ehrman find compelling. Here are the salient facts that virtually all scholars accept:

- Jesus was crucified in the year A.D. 30 (plus or minus two years).
- Paul was converted 1-3 years after Jesus' crucifixion (A.D. 31-33).
- Paul then went to the desert and then Damascus for three years: "But when God, who set me apart from my mother's womb and called me by his grace, was pleased to reveal his Son in me so that I might preach him among the Gentiles, my immediate response was not to consult any human being. I did not go up to Jerusalem to see those who were apostles before I was, but I went into Arabia. Later I returned to Damascus. Then after three years, I went up to Jerusalem...." (Galatians 1:15-18)
- After the desert and Damascus, Paul went to Jerusalem and met with Peter and James, staying 15 days (A.D. 35): "Later I returned to Damascus. Then after three years, I went up to Jerusalem to get acquainted[1] with Cephas and stayed with him fifteen days. I saw none of the other apostles—only James, the Lord's brother." (Galatians 1:17-19)
- Paul returned to Jerusalem 14 years later (A.D. 49): "Then after fourteen years, I went up again to Jerusalem, this time with Barnabas. I took Titus along also. I went in response to a revelation and, meeting privately with those esteemed as

leaders, I presented to them the gospel that I preach among the Gentiles. I wanted to be sure I was not running and had not been running my race in vain…. As for those who were held in high esteem—whatever they were makes no difference to me; God does not show favoritism—they added nothing to my message." (Galatians 2:1-2, 6)

• Paul wrote a letter to the Corinthians, summarizing the facts of the Gospel message he received (A.D. 54-55): "For what I received I passed on to you as of first importance: that Christ died for our sins according to the Scriptures, that he was buried, that he was raised on the third day according to the Scriptures…." (1 Corinthians 15:3-4)

## HOW PAUL'S ACCOUNTS LEAD BACK TO A CREED THAT WAS FORMULATED AS CLOSE AS A FEW MONTHS AFTER JESUS' CRUCIFIXION

Working backward in time, Paul wrote 1 Corinthians in A.D. 54-55. 1 Corinthians 15:3 mentions "I passed on to you…." Paul was in Corinth approximately A.D. 51. Thus, he "passed on" the fact of the resurrection in the year A.D. 51, 21 years after Jesus' crucifixion. More importantly, Paul says in 1 Corinthians 15:3, "For what I received…." The question is, "When did Paul receive the Gospel?" Although it could have been during his second visit to Jerusalem (Galatians 2:1ff) in A.D. 49, which would be a mere 19 years after Jesus' crucifixion it is more likely that Paul received the Gospel during his first visit to Jerusalem (Galatians 1:14-19) in A.D. 35, five years after Christ's crucifixion.

Paul tells the Galatians that he immediately began preaching the Gospel after his first visit to Jerusalem (see Galatians 1:21-24), which certainly must be understood to include the facts that Paul "received" that he references in 1 Corinthians 15:3). Therefore, Paul is presenting facts to the Corinthians in the years 54-55 that he heard from Peter (and possibly James, the brother of Jesus—see Galatians 1:19) in the year 35. This takes us back to within five years of Jesus' death, to information received from eyewitnesses (Peter and James).

Finally, Paul's statement in 1 Corinthians 15:3-4 is considered by most scholars to be an ancient "creed," a formulated statement of beliefs that is easy to memorize and recite. Scholars have determined that the formulation of the creed found in 1 Corinthians 15:3-4 goes back to within 2-3 year of Jesus' crucifixion,[2] with some concluding it was developed within months of Jesus' death.[3] Thus, even without the Gospels, there is substantial evidence for Jesus' death and resurrection that is virtually (by ancient history standards) contemporaneous with the presumed events. Scholars conclude from this that there was insufficient time for the core facts of the Gospel to be distorted, resolving the question of whether information in the Gospels, even if written 40-65 years after Jesus' death, is reliable.

Therefore, even if one holds to late dates for the writing of the Gospels (i.e., 40-65 years after Jesus) or rejects the accuracy of the Gospels entirely, the core facts of Christianity are supported by solid evidence in Paul's letters that originated a mere few years, and perhaps as short of time as a few months, after Jesus' death. Few facts of history enjoy such contemporaneous corroboration. As a result, skepticism of the claims of Christianity loses its luster, and the evidence in support of Christianity strongly supports the conclusion that Christianity is a thinking person's faith, based on historically verifiable facts.

## A FINAL WORD

This book defends the historical and textual reliability of the canonical Gospels, making a case for adequate certainty that the Gospels are true. The reader has been presented with substantial evidence that we have accurate, unbiased accounts for the life and teachings of Jesus of Nazareth. The Gospels, written as biographies of Jesus in the same fashion as Roman writers of the time wrote biographies of important people, provide virtually all reliable historical information about Jesus that exists today.

The investigation into the trustworthiness of the Gospel accounts is not merely a case to be solved, because the implications of the Gospel claims being true are of eternal importance. Jesus, in the Gospels, claims He came to give His life as a ransom (Matthew 20:28), and predicted that He would be crucified and rise from the dead on the third day (Matthew 16:21). He also claimed to be the only way to God (John14:6). Historical investigation brings us to evidence, from the Gospel accounts and extra-biblical sources, that confirms Jesus lived, died on a cross, and rose from the dead. But it is beyond the ability of history to confirm that trusting in Jesus' death for forgiveness of sins confers eternal life on those who believe.

The evidence in the Gospels will lead to the cross of Christ, where a sinless man died a horrible death so that He might save a lost humanity. But the fact of Jesus' death is not intended to be merely an academic conclusion to which we give a nod because of the compelling evidence that it truly happened. Jesus died so that by believing in Him we will be set free. Historical investigation cannot prove that those who trust in Jesus are forgiven, but it can provide a factual, logical, reasonable basis for believing.

When Jesus told the paralyzed man that his sins were forgiven (Matthew 9:2ff), then healed the man, it was a combination of a verifiable event (the healing) and a truth claim (Jesus stating He can forgive sin). Those present in that house observed the healing, but the forgiveness was not something visible. In the same way, we can observe history through the Gospels, but the forgiveness Jesus offers in the Gospels must be accepted by faith. Not blind faith, which means believing without evidence or regardless of contrary evidence, but faith founded on fact, as with the paralyzed man who had good reason to believe his sins were forgiven because he had been miraculously healed.

The case for the reliability of the Gospels gives all people a rational basis for putting trust in the One who is presented in the Gospels as the crucified, risen Son of God. Jesus said to those who believed in Him, "Because I live, you also will live" (John 14:19). This book is intended to provide reasons to believe, so that the readers, too, "will live," just like the stated reason for why John wrote his Gospel, "that you may believe that Jesus is the Messiah, the Son of God, and that by believing you may have life in his name" (John 20:31).

# END NOTES

## INTRODUCTION
## END NOTES

[1]C. S. Lewis, "Christian Apologetics," 1945, included in *God in the Dock,* (Grand Rapids: Eerdmans, 1970), 101-102.

[2]Craig A. Evans, *Fabricating Jesus* (Downers Grove, Illinois: InterVarsity, 2006), 46.

[3]L. T. Johnson, *The Real Jesus: The Misguided Quest for the Historical Jesus and the Truth of the Traditional Gospels,* (San Francisco: HarperSanFrancisco, 1996), 85.

[4]Michael R. Licona, *The Resurrection of Jesus* (Downers Grove, Illinois: InterVarsity Press, 2010), 69.

[5]The age-old question of why there is a universe has been raised as far back as Aristotle, and its modern version of "why is there something rather than nothing?" was popularized by 17th century philosopher Gottfried Leibniz.

[6]Job 14:14 in the Bible. Job's question takes the more philosophical issue raised by Leibniz and narrows it to the more practical question of whether this life is all there is. Christianity answers the question by pointing to Jesus' teaching "He who believes in Me has eternal life" (John 6:47), and Jesus' resurrection from the dead as evidence that Jesus's claim is true.

## CHAPTER ONE
## END NOTES

[1]Murray J. Harris, *Raised Immortal: Resurrection and Immortality in the New Testament* (Grand Rapids: Eerdmans, 1985), 68.

[2]Gary Habermas, "Recent Perspectives on the Reliability of the Gospels," Christian Research Journal, vol. 28, number 1, 2005.

[3]Habermas, *id.*

[4]David Hackett Fisher, *Historian's Fallacies: Toward a Logic of Historical Thought* (New York: Harper and Row, 1970), 62.

[5]In common law, *prima facie* refers to evidence in support of a claim that is sufficient to prove the claim unless rebutted. A *prima facie* case effectively shifts the burden to the party disputing the claim.

[6]*Burden of proof* refers to a situation where there is a factual dispute, and identifies the side of the argument that must first make a factual showing ("prima facie case") in support of the argument before the case can go forward, and before the other side is required to rebut the evidence. In criminal cases, the burden is on the prosecution to show, beyond reasonable doubt, that the accused committed each element of the offense charged. Once the prosecution meets its burden, the defense may present evidence and argument to rebut the prosecution's case. In civil cases, the plaintiff bears the burden of proof, and the standard is generally whether its claims are "more likely than not" (i.e., the "preponderance of the evidence"). As with criminal cases, in civil matters, once a plaintiff has made an affirmative showing, i.e., met its burden of proof, the defendant presents evidence and arguments to rebut the claims of the plaintiff.

[7]Ancient documents that had dates were not dated in the same manner as today. If ancient documents were dated, the date would not be a numbered year, such as 2017, but would typically be in reference to a king, ruler or elected official's reign, such as "in the third year of Herod's reign." Our current dating system marks time from the birth of Jesus, as first developed in the 6th century by a Scythian monk, Dionysius Exiguus. The common designation A.D., standing for *Anno Domini* ("year of the Lord") has been gradually replaced by "CE" standing for "Common Era" with "BCE" ("before Common Era") an alternative to B.C. ("before Christ"). At the time of Jesus some Roman historians used the "AUC" method of dating, standing for *ab urbe condita,* a reference to the founding of Rome in 753

B.C. (based on the etiological myth of Romulus and Remus). More common during Jesus' time was dating events by linking them to the names of the Roman consuls at the time of the events (*consul* was the highest elected office in Rome, and each year two consuls were elected to one-year terms). A list of Roman consuls was maintained, so linking their names to the time of an event identified the Roman year the event occurred.

[8]Acts 11:28 and 18:2.

[9]As reported by 5th century writer Paulus Orosius, who bases the date on a non-extant report from Josephus. Roman historian Suetonius confirms the expulsion, but does not narrow the event beyond the reign of Claudius.

[10]The technical term is *terminus post quem,* the "earliest possible date" for something.

[11]Cf. R. Riesner, *Paul's Early Period: Chronology, Mission Strategy, Theology* (Grand Rapids: Eerdmans, 1998).

[12]The technical term is *terminus ante quem,* the "latest possible date" for something.

[13]Some scholars contend that John's Gospel was written by several people, at different times, with the later authors adding to the initial core document. An often-cited example is John chapter 21, which is thought by some to be an "add-on" to the presumed ending found in chapter 20. See George R. Beasely-Murray, *John,* 2nd ed.; World Bible Commentary 36 (Columbia: Thomas Nelson, 1999), 395, and John Breck, "John 21: Appendix, Epilogue or Conclusion? In *St. Vladimir's Theological Quarterly* 36, 1992, 27-49 for discussions of the John 21 issue. For a response to the challenges to John 21's authenticity, see Craig L. Blomberg, *The Historical Reliability of John's Gospel* (Downers Grove: InterVarsity Press, 2001), 272.

[14]E.g., testimony from Irenaeus, the Muratorian Canon, Tatian's *Diatessaron,* anti-Marcionite prologues.

[15]Scholars who accept a date later than A.D. 70 for John's Gospel have various explanations for the silence on the

destruction of Jerusalem and the temple, including the contention that it was written long enough *after* A.D. 70 (e.g., A.D. 90-95) that there was no need to further elaborate on those dark days in Jewish and Christian history.

[16]Ferdinand Christian Baur, *Kritische Untersuchungen über die kanonischen Evangelien* (Tübingen: Verlag und Druck, 1847), 239.

[17]*Higher criticism* refers to questions regarding the sources and literary genre of a work of literature. Sometimes called "historical criticism," or "historical-critical method," higher criticism is a branch of "literary criticism" that deals with the evaluation and interpretation of literature, including an author's goals and methods. Higher criticism became virtually synonymous with "biblical criticism" in the 18th century, and has since been further refined into subcategories of *form criticism, redaction criticism* and *literary criticism.* For a helpful, though technical, discussion of these subcategories as applied to the Gospels, see Craig L. Blomberg, *The Historical Reliability of the Gospels,* 2nd ed. (Downers Grove, Ill: Inter-Varsity 2007), 48-103. "Lower criticism" refers to *textual criticism,* the reconstructing of the original wording of literature where the original manuscripts are lost. Textual criticism examines existing manuscripts of the literature, translations of the literature, and references outside of the literature to arrive at the likely wording of the original text.

[1425]E.g, Donald Scholtz, *Jesus in the Gospels and Acts: Introducing the New Testament* (Saint Mary's Press, 2009), 34-35, building on the notion that Mark wrote around A.D. 70, and that Matthew followed Mark. Also, some scholars view Jesus' prediction of the destruction of the temple (Matthew 24:1-2) as actually looking back on the destruction of the temple, which occurred in A.D. 70, resulting in the conclusion that Matthew's Gospel should be dated 80 or later. The position that Matthew 24:1-2 is describing an historical event as if it were yet to happen suggests that either the adherents of the view cannot accept a miraculous prophetic ability on Jesus' part, or else they believe the writer of Matthew fabricated the account for some reason. Either view is weakened by the fact that throughout Matthew the temple is still standing (cf. Matthew 5:23-24; 17:24-27; 23:16-22).

[26]Eusebius, *Church History*, 5.8.2.

[27]Eusebius, *Church History*, 3.39.14-17.

[28]Daniel B. Wallace, *Matthew: Introduction, Argument, and Outline*, from series, "New Testament Introductions and Outlines, bible.org, retrieved September 7, 2016.

[29]R. T. France, *The Gospel of Mark*, New International Greek Testament Commentary (Grand Rapids: Eerdmans, 2002), 38.

[30]Craig S. Keener, *A Commentary on the Gospel of Matthew* (Grand Rapids: Eerdmans, 1999), 42-43.

[31]Eusebius, *Church History*, 3.39.15.

[32]Eusebius, *Church History,* 3.39.14-15.

[33]Eusebius, *Church History*, 2.15.1-2. Clement says Peter verified Mark's account.

[34]*Against Heresies,* 3.1.2.

[35]*De Viris Illustribus*, viii (ca 392-393). Later tradition holds that Mark was martyred in A.D. 68.

[36]James Crossley argues that the *latest* dating for Mark's Gospel is A.D. 45, and holds that Mark was most likely written between the late 30s and early 40s C.E, *The Date of Mark's Gospel: Insight from the Law in Earliest Christianity* (London: T&T Clark/Continuum, 2004).

[37]D. A. Carson and Douglas Moo, *An Introduction to the New Testament*, 2nd ed. (Grand Rapids: Zondervan, 2005), 179-182. Carson and Moo conclude that Luke used Mark as a source (cf. Luke 1:1-4), and since they conclude Luke was likely written in the early 60s, Mark must have been written several years earlier.

[38]France, ibid. 5-19.

[39]Bart D. Ehrman, *The New Testament: A Historical Introduction to the Early Christian Writings*, 4th ed (Oxford: Oxford University Press, 2008), 90.

[40]Robert H. Stein, *Mark,* Evangelical Commentary of the New Testament (Grand Rapids: Baker, 2008), 12-15.

[41]E.g., Rainer Riesner, *Paul's Early Period: Chronology, Mission, Strategy, Theology,* Grand Rapids: Eerdmans, 1998.

[42]E.g., J. A. Fitzmeyer, *The Gospel According to Luke* (I-IX). AB 28 (Garden City, NY: Doubleday, 1981), 1:53-57.

[43]Carson and Moo, ibid. 207-210.

[44]Darrell Bock, *Luke 1:1-9:50,* Baker Exegetical Commentary on the New Testament (Grand Rapids: Baker, 1994), 18.

[45]W. G. Kümmel, *The New Testament: The History of the Investigation of Its Problems* (New York: Abingdon, 1970), 151.

[46]The text reads εστιν δε εν τοισ Ιεροσολυμοισ (*estin de en tois Ierosolumois*). New Testament scholar Dan Wallace points out that the Greek verb *eimi* (in John 5:2 the verb is a third person singular, present active indicative, commonly translated "[it] is") that begins this clause "is nowhere else clearly used as a historical present" and, therefore, "the present tense should be taken as indicating present time from the viewpoint of the speaker." He adds, "The implication of this seems to be that this Gospel was written before the destruction of Jerusalem in 70 CE." Daniel B. Wallace, *Greek Grammar Beyond the Basics* (Grand Rapids: Eerdmans, 1996), 531.

[47]Daniel B. Wallace, *The Gospel of John: Introduction, Argument, Outline,* from series, "New Testament Introductions and Outlines, bible.org, retrieved September 7, 2016.

[48]Leon Morris, *The Gospel According to John* (Grand Rapids, Eerdmans, 1971), 30-35

[49]D. A. Carson, *The Gospel According to John,* Pillar New Testament Commentary (Grand Rapids: Eerdmans, 1991), 268.

[50]James D. G. Dunn, *Christology in the Making: A New Testament Inquiry into the Origins of the Doctrine of the Incarnation,* 2nd ed. (Grand Rapids: Eerdmans, 1996), 213-238. Dunn's late dating derives from his conclusion that John's Gospel has a developed Christology that is not present in the Synoptics, requiring a later date to account for the time necessary for the development of the theology found in John.

[51]Irenaeus (130-202), quoted by Eusebius, *Church History,* 3.23.3-4, states that John died during the reign of Roman Emperor Trajan, A.D. 98-117; Jerome (347-420) writes, *Vir. ill.*9, that John died in the 68th year after Jesus' passion, i.e., A.D. 98-101.

[52]Originally called "the Atkinson-Schiffrin memory model." See Richard Atkinson & R.M. Shiffrin, "Human memory: A proposed system and its control processes" in K. W. Spence and J. T. Spence eds., *The Psychology of Learning and Motivation,* vol. 8 (London: Academic Press, 1968). Today the model for quantifying long-term memory and recall is "Search of Associative Memory" ("SAM"). See J. G. Raaijmakers & Richard Shiffrin, 1980, "SAM: A theory of probabilistic search of associative memory" in G. H. Bower, ed., *The Psychology of Learning and Motivation,* vol. 14, 207-262. New York: Academic Press, 1980.

[53]Roger Brown and James Kulik, Flashbulb memories. *Cognition* 5 (1): 73–99, 1977.

[54]Mara Mather and Laura L. Carstensen, "Aging and motivated cognition: The positivity effect in attention and memory." *Trends in Cognitive Sciences,* Vol 9, Issue 10, October 2005, 496-502.

[55]Brown & Kulik, ibid.

[56]Elizabeth A. Kensinger, *Remembering the Details: Effects of Emotion,* [Emot. Rev. 1, 99–113. 10.1177/1754073908100432], 2009.

[57]See Michael R. Licona, *Why Are There Differences in the Gospels?* (Oxford University Press, 2017) for an in-depth analysis of

literary conventions used in ancient biographies compared with the Gospels. Licona asserts "Greaco-Roman biography was a broad and flexible genre." (p. 5) He then spends nearly 100 pages analyzing parallel accounts in Plutarch's *Lives* after which he compares them to parallel accounts in the Gospels. Licona's conclusion is that the Gospels use similar types of compositional devices as Plutarch (p. 182), which includes creatively reconstructing peripheral details of an event in efforts to write a quality narrative (p. 184).

[58]Greek εξορυσσω (*exorusso*), "to excavate."

[59]Greek κεραμων (*keramon*) "clay tiles."

[60]Craig A. Evans, *Luke* (Hendricksen: Peabody, 1990), 91-92

[61]Many verses in the Synoptic Gospels (i.e., Matthew, Mark and Luke) are word-for-word the same, and these three Gospels frequently follow the same order of events. Efforts to explain these similarities fall under the heading, "Synoptic Problem." The obvious literary dependence within the Synoptics has led scholars to conclude either that two of the Synoptics are dependent on the third, or that there is a missing document that is a common source for two or all three Synoptics. The problem with the "dependent on another Gospel" theory is determining whether Matthew relied on Mark, or vice versa. The unanimous view of early Christians such as Augustine was that Matthew wrote first. Modern arguments in support of Matthew's priority were popularized by Johann Griesbach (d. 1812). However, most scholars today hold to the "priority of Mark." For a summary of the various approaches to the "Synoptic Problem," see Craig L. Blomberg, *The Historical Reliability of the Gospels,* 2d ed (Downers Grove, Ill: Inter-Varsity 2007), 37-47.

[62]See my essay "Inspiration" that discusses *ipsissima vox* ("authentic voice") compared to *ipsissima verba* ("authentic words") when considering how the words of Jesus are conveyed in the Gospels. Johnmarkstewart.blogspot.com, February 13, 2010.

[63]The "source" that many scholars postulate Matthew, Mark and Luke used is referred to as the "Q" document, from the first letter of the German word for "source" (*quelle*). Although no such document has ever been discovered, scholars put forward reasonable arguments in support of its existence.

[64]"The primary sources written by people who actually knew Alexander or who gathered info from men who served with Alexander are all lost (except for a few inscriptions and fragments)" Peter Green, *Alexander of Macedon, 356-323 B.C.: A Historical Biography* (University of California Press, 1992), xxxiii. An example is Alexander's biographer, Callisthenes of Olynthus, who journeyed with Alexander during his military campaigns. It is unclear how long after the events the accounts were written. His writings exist only in a few fragments.

[65]Arrian relies on Alexander's officer Aristobulus, an eyewitness to Alexander's campaigns, and Ptolemy, a close friend and bodyguard of Alexander who became king of Egypt following Alexander's death. Philosopher Plutarch presents the life of Alexander through a moral lens, and his writing about Alexander reveals that he was familiar with many sources that chronicled the life of Alexander.

Roman historian Curtius Diodorus of Sicily, sometime between 60 and 30 B.C., wrote 10 volumes covering the period from the Trojan War to the death of Alexander the Great, but only six of the volumes survive intact. He is not considered a reliable historian for the details of Alexander's life. Diodorus relied on the works of Cleitarchus, who wrote a decade or so after the time of Alexander, and Hieronymus of Cardia, a contemporary of Alexander the Great. None of the writings of Cleitarchus or Hieronymus survive. Diodorus' *History of Alexander* "sometimes sacrifices historical reliability to keep the story entertaining," to the point that "modern historians prefer the account of Arrian…." (Jona Lendering, *Cleitarchus*, at livius.org). Quintus Curtius Rufus wrote 10 volumes on the life of Alexander, based largely on Cleitarchus, of which the last eight survive. His real subject was not even Alexander, but rather the tyranny of Tiberius and Caligula, and his books show a limited knowledge, at best, of geography, chronology and military knowledge. Jona Lendering, *Curtius,* at livius. org. Justin, a Latin historian of whom little is known, wrote The *Epitome of the Philippic History of Pompeius Trogus* in the 2nd century A.D. condensing the works of an earlier history by Trogus from the 1st century A.D.

[66]E.g., When Arrian and Diodorus chronicle Alexander's crossing of the Hellespont on his way to attacking the Persians, they have two different, irreconcilable accounts of when and where the attack took place. Arrian says the attack took place immediately upon Alexander's arrival at the Granicus River, whereas Diodorus wrote that the attack did not take place until dawn the next day. No one uses these discrepancies to conclude that either the authors were biased, totally unreliable, or, even more absurd, that Alexander the Great never lived. It is unfortunate that many critical scholars do not afford the same benefit of the doubt to the New Testament accounts of Jesus.

[67]F. F. Bruce, *The New Testament Documents—are they reliable?* (Grand Rapids: Eerdmans, 5th rev ed., 1960), 45.

## CHAPTER TWO
## END NOTES

[1]John 20:30-31, "Jesus performed many other signs in the presence of his disciples, which are not recorded in this book. But these are written that you may believe that Jesus is the Messiah, the Son of God, and that by believing you may have life in his name."

[2]John 21:24, "This is the disciple who testifies to these things and who wrote them down. We know that his testimony is true."

[3]E.g., Albert Schweitzer, *The Quest of the Historical Jesus,* published in German in 1913 as *Geschichte der Leben-Jesu-Forschung* and in English in 2001 as *The Quest of the Historical Jesus,* trans. John Bowden, et al. 2nd ed. (Minneapolis: Fortress Press).

[4]Richard Burridge. *What Are the Gospels? A Comparison with Graeco-Roman Biography* (Cambridge: Cambridge University Press, 1992).

[5]Burridge, following Wittgenstein's "family resemblance theory," shows statistically that the amount of time spent on Jesus' death, the percentage of verbs having the hero as the subject, and the percentage of verbs found in the hero's sayings are consistent with the percentages of these found in Graeco-Roman biographies. These concentrations, common to the Gospels and other ancient biographies, are found in no other genre of ancient literature.

[6]*Ancient bioi* is the technical term Burridge uses for the genre of ancient Graeco-Roman biography.

[7]Recently, some scholars have attempted to show that the Gospels may have taken existing historical fiction and replaced the hero of the stories with Jesus. For example, writer Dennis R. McDonald claims that Mark's Gospel took stories from Homer's *Iliad* and *Odyssey* and turned them into stories about Jesus. Dennis R. MacDonald, *Homeric Epics and the Gospel of Mark* (New Haven: Yale University Press, 2000). The formal term for imitating another writer's style is *mimesis*. Imitating a style of a historical fiction writer such as Homer does not prove that the imitator's work is also fiction. An author can use any number of literary devices to convey history to the writer's intended audience. Many writers find MacDonald's general thesis unpersuasive (e.g., http://www.tektonics.org/gk/homer-mark.php), including his argument that Judas Iscariot and Mary Magdalene never existed (see http://ronaldvhuggins.blogspot.com/2016/04/did-judas-exist-friendly-critique-of.html)

[8]Justin, writing in Greek, used the word *apomnemoneuemata* (απομνημονευματα) twice in *First Apology* (ca 155) and 13 times in *Dialogue with Trypho* (ca 160). German scholar Martin Hengel, late professor at Tübingen, wrote: "The ancient reader will probably have been well aware of the differences in style and education, say, between Mark and Xenophon; but he

will also have noticed what the gospels had in common with the literature of biographical 'reminiscences' – and unlike the majority of German New Testament scholars today, he did not mind at all regarding the evangelists as authors of biographical reminiscences of Jesus which went back to the disciples of Jesus themselves." *Acts and the History of Earliest Christianity* (Philadelphia: Fortress, 1980), 29.

[9]Investigators traced the Vehicle Identification Number ("VIN") on the rear axle of the Ryder truck used in the Oklahoma City bombing to a Junction City, Kansas location where the truck was rented. Workers there described the person who rented the truck to an FBI artist, who made a sketch that was circulated in the area. A local motel manager recognized Timothy McVeigh from the sketch, which led to his arrest. Prosecutors secured a murder conviction essentially based on circumstantial evidence that McVeigh was at the scene of the bombing. The evidence included his using his real name at the Kansas motel, the Ryder truck axle found at the scene of the bombing, and testimony that McVeigh rented the Ryder truck. Prosecutors also had testimony from Michael Fortier, whom McVeigh told about his plan to bomb a federal building in Oklahoma City, and McVeigh's fingerprint on a receipt used to buy some of the material used to make the bomb.

[10]Originally published in 1818, now in the public domain.

[11]Craig S. Keener, *Miracles: The Credibility of the New Testament Accounts,* 2 vols. (Grand Rapids: Baker Academic, 2011).

[12]Within the text of the Gospels the writers are not named, just as many writers contemporary with the canonical Gospels, e.g., Suetonius and Plutarch, did not include their names within the text.

[13]Since the original Gospel writings ("autographs") are missing, there is no way to be certain whether the original Gospels did or did not have a "cover page" that identified the writer. However, some scholars present arguments for the original Gospels having a title page that appear to shift the burden

back to the skeptic, including the position that anonymous Gospels would not have survived without being attributed to a reputable source. See D.A. Carson and Douglas J. Moo, *An Introduction to the New Testament,* 2nd ed. (Grand Rapids: Zondervan, 2005), 140; see also Nancy Pardee, referencing Martin Hengel, *The Genre of the Didache: A Text-Linguistic Analysis* (Dissertation, University of Chicago, 2002), 113.

[14]Daniel B. Wallace, "New Testament Introduction and Outlines," "Matthew: Introduction, Argument and Outline," 1, https://bible.org/seriespage/1-matthew-introduction-argument-and-outline, retrieved September 15, 2016.

[15]Donald Guthrie, *New Testament Introduction,* 3rd ed. rev. (Downers Grove: Inter-Varsity, 1970), 33, referencing, inter alia, G. D. Kilpatrick, *The Origins of the Gospel According to St. Matthew (1946),* 136.

[16]E.g., P66, part of the Bodmer Papyri collection (named after the Swiss collector who acquired it in the mid-20th c.) is a near complete copy of the Gospel of John and at the beginning it lists John as the author. The codex is typically assigned a date of A.D. 200. P[75], ca 200, is also part of the Bodmer Papyri, and it, too, contains the beginning of John's Gospel, listing John as the author. The fact is that no extant manuscript of the canonical Gospels that contains the beginning of the text fails to name one of the traditional writers as the author.

[17]www.reasonablefaith.org/gospel-authorship-who-cares, Q & A with William Lane Craig #373, June 8, 2014, "Gospel Authorship—Who Cares?" retrieved September 13, 2016.

[18]Ibid. Craig's factors are: (1) Historical congruence (consistency with known historical facts, (2) Independent, early attestation (the saying or event appears in multiple sources from a time near to the occurrence of the alleged saying or event that are not dependent on each other or a common source, (3) Embarrassment (a saying or event that puts the source of the information in a negative light, i.e., not the kind of saying or story a writer would make up), (4) Dissimilarity (departs from

prevailing thought forms), (5) Semitisms (accounts contain Aramaic or Hebrew expressions or roots), and (6) Coherence (consistent with established facts about Jesus).

[19]*Apologeticus* 16, ca 200. Tacitus wrote two major works, *Histories* and *Annals* in ca A.D. 105 and 116, respectively. Pliny the Younger (ca 105) wrote to Tacitus and mentions that Tacitus was writing a *Historiae,* which likely referred to a general category of historical writing rather than Tacitus' actual *Histories,* although this is not certain. Thus, Tertullian's reference (ca 220) to Tacitus' writing *Histories* is generally considered the earliest *direct* attribution to *Histories.*

[20]Papius, ca A.D. 95-120, references that Matthew and Mark wrote Gospels. Irenaeus, ca. 180, references that Luke and John wrote Gospels. Irenaeus, as a student of Polycarp (69-155) who had been a disciple of John the Apostle, was in a favorable position to confirm authorship of John's Gospel.

[21]According to Irenaeus (125-202), *Against Heresies* 5.33.4, ca A.D. 180, quoted by Eusebius, *History of the Church* 3.39.1.

[22]Eusebius, *History of the Church,* 3.39.16.

[23]*Against Heresies* 3.1.1.

[24]Eusebius, *History of the Church,* 3.39.15.

[25]Justin Martyr, *Dialogue with Trypho the Jew,* 106.3.

[26]Bart Ehrman, *Forgery and Counterforgery: The Use of Literary Deceit in Early Christian Polemics* (Oxford Academic, 2012). It must be emphasized, in view of Ehrman's position, that the Gospel of Peter does *not* give an account of Jesus naming Peter and the sons of Zebedee.

[27]Justin Martyr, *Dialogue with Trypho the Jew,* 103.8.

[28]Walter Richard Cassels, *Supernatural Religion: An Inquiry,* 6th ed. (Toronto and Detroit: Rose-Belford, 1879), 254.

[29]Justin Martyr, *1 Apology* 66:3.

[30]Irenaeus, *Against Heresies,* 3.1.1.

[31]The 7th century manuscript known as the Muratorian Canon (or, "Muratorian Fragment") is the oldest known list of books of the New Testament, and is a 7th century Latin manuscript. Certain features of the canon indicate it was translated from a Greek manuscript written around the year A.D. 170 because it references Pius I, Bishop of Rome (142-157) as being in Rome "very recently." The author of the Muratorian Canon was aware of four Gospels, naming Luke and John, although the names of first two Gospels at the beginning of the list are not included because the beginning of the fragment is missing. It was discovered by an Italian historian Ludovico Muratori (1672-1750) and, hence, bears his name.

[32]Tertullian, *Against Marcion*, 4.2.1-5.

[33]Irenaeus, *Against Heresies*, 3.1.1

[34]Köstenberger, 2001b: 17-47). Cited in *John: Baker Exegetical Commentary on the New Testament* (Grand Rapids: Baker Publishing Group, 2004), 7: "I have shown that the apostolic paradigm was challenged on largely philosophical rather than evidential grounds and that there is therefore compelling reason to doubt that the Fourth Gospel's Johannine authorship has ever been refuted by actual argument."

[35]Textual critic Bart Ehrman uses the variety in the titles of the canonical Gospels, e.g., "Gospel according to Mark" (ευαγ–γελιον κατα Μαρκον), "Gospel of Jesus Christ according to Mark" (το ευαγγελιον Ιησου Χριστου κατα Μαρκον) as evidence that "their familiar names do not go back to a single 'original' title, but were added by later scribes." (*Jesus: Apocalyptic Prophet of the New Millennium* (Oxford: Oxford University Press, 1999), 249-250. What Ehrman fails to acknowledge is that attribution to the traditional writers by Papias, Irenaeus and others provides a seamless tradition that goes back to the apostles themselves. Thus, Ehrman's "evidence" begs the question of who wrote the Gospels, does not answer whether the writers' names appeared in the originals, and, if they didn't, does not account for how the traditional writers' names became affixed.

Other critics contend that the attribution to the traditional writers is suspect because the titles are not in the genitive case, e.g., "Gospel *of* Mark" (ευαγγελιον του Μαρκου) as is common with many ancient texts, but, instead, use "Gospel *according to* Mark" (ευαγγελιον κατα Μαρκον), using the preposition *kata* ("according to"). This argument is unconvincing, as Arndt and Gingrich indicate in their lexicon that κατα "Sometimes...acts as the periphrasis of a possessive pronoun or a genitive...Here also belongs the titles of the gospels ευαγγελιον κατα ΜατΘαιον, etc., where κατα is likewise paraphrasis for a genitive." William F. Arndt and F. Wilbur Gingrich, *A Greek-English Lexicon of the New Testament and Other Early Christian Literature*, 4th ed. (Chicago: University of Chicago Press, 1952), 406-407. For a contrary view, see Matthew Ferguson, "Why Scholars Doubt the Traditional Authors of the Gospels, _ https://adversusapologetica.wordpress.com/2013/12/17/why-scholars-doubt-the-traditional-authors-of-the-gospels/

[36]Justin Martyr, *1 Apologies* and *Dialogue with Trypho the Jew.*

[37]Dom Donatien De Bruyne, "Les plus anciens prologues latins des Evangiles," *Revue Benedictine,* XL, 1928, 193-214.

[38]Adolph von Harnack, "Die altesten Evangelien-Prologe und die Bildung des Neuen Testaments," (Sitzungsberichte der Preuss, Akademie der Wissenschaften, phil-hist Klasse, XXIV, 1928), 322ff.

[39]E.g., Engelbert Gutwenger, *The Anti-Marcionite Prologues*, cdn.theologicalstudies.net, retrieved June 26, 2016

[40]C.M. Tuckett, "The Didache" in *The Reception of the New Testament in the Apostolic Fathers,* A. F. Gregory and C. M. Tuckett, eds. (Oxford: Oxford University Press, 2005), 126.

[41]Most scholars accept seven letters attributed to Ignatius as authentic because Church historian Eusebius mentions seven and Origen mentions two. Six additional letters attributed to Ignatius are generally regarded as spurious.

[42]H. H. Drake Williams III, *Jesus Tried and True* (Eugene, Oregon: Wipf & Stock, 2013), 73.

[43]H. R. Drobner, *The Fathers of the Church: A Comprehensive Introduction* (Peabody, MA: Hendrickson, 2007), 50.

[44]C.E. Hill, *The Johannine Corpus in the Early Church* (Oxford: Oxford University Press, 2004), 442.

[45]J. B. Lightfoot, *The Apostolic Fathers* (Grand Rapids: Baker, 1956), 2.2.224.

[46]*Gegraptai* (γεγραπται) in Greek.

[47]Sir William Ramsay, *St. Paul the Traveller and the Roman Citizen* (London: Hodder & Stroughton, 1925), 4.

[48]Colin J. Hemer, *The Book of Acts in the Setting of Hellenistic History,* ed. C. H. Gempf (Tübingen: Mohr, 1989).

[49]See William Hendriksen, *Exposition of the Gospel According to John, New Testament Commentary* (Grand Rapids: Baker, 1953), 3-31; Donald Guthrie, *New Testament Introduction*, 3rd ed. (Inter-Varsity: Downers Grove, Illinois, 1970), 258-271

## CHAPTER THREE
### END NOTES

[1]"Bias" involves "prejudice in favor of or against one thing, person or group compared with another, usually in a way considered to be unfair." "Prejudice" involves a "preconceived opinion that is not based on reason or actual experience." https:/www.Google.com#q=bias; https://www.google.com/#q=prejudice

[2]Judicial Council of California Criminal Jury Instructions (CALCRIM) 2016, No. 226 regarding witnesses.

[3]Flavius Josephus, *Antiquities of the Jews,* 18.63-64: "At this time there appeared Jesus, a wise man [ ]. For he was a doer of amazing deeds, a teacher of persons who receive truth with pleasure. He won over many Jews and many of the Greeks. [ ] And when Pilate condemned him to the cross, the leading men among us having accused him, those who loved him from the first did

not cease to do so. [ ] And to the present tribe of Christians, named after this person, has not disappeared." (Brackets indicate omitted sections that are found in manuscripts of Josephus' *Antiquities* but appear to be later interpolations.) *Antiquities* 20:200-201: "He [Ananus] convened the council of judges and brought before it the brother of Jesus--the one called 'Christ'--whose name was James, and certain others."

[4]See Louis H. Feldman, *Studies in Josephus' Rewritten Bible* (Brill: Leiden, 1998).

[5]Jim Bloom, *Josephus as a Source for a Military History of the Jewish Revolt*. An abridgment of an address to the military classics seminar, Fort Meyer, Virginia, September 19, 2000. http://www.josephus.org/FlJosephus2/bloomRevolt.htm

[6]Irenaeus (130-202), quoted by Eusebius, *Church History* 3.23.3-4, states that John died during the reign of Roman Emperor Trajan, 98-117; Jerome (347-420) writes, *Vir. ill.*9, that John died in the 68th year after Jesus' passion, i.e., A.D. 98-101

[7]Gerd Lüdemann, *What Really Happened to Jesus?* Trans. John Bowden (Louisville, Kentucky: John Knox Press, 1995), 80.

[8]Bruce M. Metzger, *A Textual Commentary on the Greek New Testament* (London: United Bible Societies, 1971), 219-222.

[9]Luke 2:1-5 references a decree that went out from Caesar Augustus "while Quirinius was governor of Syria" (Luke 2:2). Many critical scholars consider this an error, because Roman and Jewish sources list others as governor of Syria during the period leading up to the birth of Jesus. These sources place Quirinius as governor from A.D. 6-9. Conservative scholars have proposed many possible explanations to challenge the critics' conclusion that Luke is wrong. See Craig L. Blomberg, *The Historical Reliability of John's Gospel* (Downers Grove: InterVarsity Press, 2001), 248-249 and Darrell L. Bock, *Luke 1:1-9:50,* Grand Rapids: Baker, 1994, 903-909.

[10]Robert W. Funk, Roy W. Hoover, and the Jesus Seminar, *The Five Gospels: What Did Jesus Really Say?* (New York: MacMillan, 1993), Introduction: "Eighty-two percent of the

words ascribed to Jesus in the gospels were not actually spoken by him, according to the Jesus Seminar."

[11]John Dominic Crossan, *Jesus: A Revolutionary Biography* (New York: Harper Collins, 1995), 145.

[12]John P. Meier, *A Marginal Jew: Rethinking the Historical Jesus,* vol. 1 (New York: Yale University Press, 1991). Meier lists several criteria for authenticity, including the "criterion of embarrassment, 168-177.

[13]Robert Funk, *Honest to Jesus: Jesus for a New Millennium* (San Francisco: Harper, 1996), 223.

[14]California Evidence Code §1200 defines the hearsay rule. "(a) "Hearsay evidence" is evidence of a statement that was made other than by a witness while testifying at the hearing and that is offered to prove the truth of the matter stated. (b) Except as provided by law, hearsay evidence is inadmissible. (c) This section shall be known and may be cited as the hearsay rule."

[15]California Evidence Code §1230: "Evidence of a statement by a declarant having sufficient knowledge of the subject is not made inadmissible by the hearsay rule if the declarant is unavailable as a witness and the statement, when made, was so far contrary to the declarant's pecuniary or proprietary interest, or so far subjected him to the risk of civil or criminal liability, or so far tended to render invalid a claim by him against another, or created such a risk of making him an object of hatred, ridicule, or social disgrace in the community, that a reasonable man in his position would not have made the statement unless he believed it to be true."

[16]California Evidence Code §1230, ibid.

## CHAPTER FOUR
## END NOTES

[1]We will use the term "lost gospels" synonymously with "non-canonical writings about Jesus," or "extra-biblical writings about Jesus," meaning all early so-called "gospels" other than Matthew, Mark, Luke, and John. The term is not meant

to confirm that these spurious writings qualify as "gospels" in the strict sense.

[2]E.g., Michael Kruger, *The Question of Canon* (Downers Grove: InterVarsity Press, 2013); Craig A. Evans, *Fabricating Jesus* (Downers Grove: InterVarsity Press, 2006).

[3]For possible motivations behind forgeries (i.e., writings falsely attributed to someone who was not the actual author) see Bruce M. Metzger, *Literary Forgeries and Canonical Pseudepigrapha*, Journal of Biblical Literature, vol. 91, No. 1, March 1972, 3-24. Metzger makes a distinction between *pseudepigrapha* and *forgeries*, but this distinction does not elevate either category to the level of being historically-reliable.

[4]Gnostics believed that the material world was evil, created by an evil being that was far removed from the transcendent, spiritual God. Gnostics believed they were enlightened by *gnosis*, the Greek word for "knowledge," which Gnostics considered as equal to salvation. Gnosticism had a profound negative influence on the Early Church, and many Christian apologists and theologians (e.g., Irenaeus, Justin Martyr) wrote refutations of Gnosticism, which emerged as a Christian heresy early in the 2nd century (Paul's letter to the Colossians addresses false beliefs that eventually became full-blown Gnosticism in the 2nd century).

[5]A category that Church historian Eusebius (ca 340) called *homologoumena* ("agreement"), *History of the Church*, 3:2.

[6]Eusebius refers to them as *antilegomena* ("spoken against"), *History of the Church*, 3:3, 5. These included Hebrews (due to the author's being anonymous), James (due to what some perceived as teachings about faith and works that contradicted justification by faith alone), 2 Peter (because it incorporates much of the Epistle of Jude, including a reference to an Old Testament-era pseudepigraphon, 1 *Enoch*), 2 John (too short in some people's minds) 3 John (too short, also) Jude (quotes from Old Testament-era pseudepigraphon 1 *Enoch*) and Revelation (due to the doctrine of *chiliasm*, meaning a

1,000-year period, commonly called the *millennium*). There were also some non-canonical writings in Eusebius' list of *antilegomena,* including the *Gospel of Hebrews, Apocalypse of Peter, Acts of Paul, Shepherd of Hermas,* the *Epistle of Barnabas* and the *Didache.* The *antilegomena* were read widely in the Early Church.

[7]The most popular was *Shepherd of Hermas.* Others included the *Didache, First Epistle of Clement, Epistle of Barnabas, Second Clement,* and *Apocalypse of Peter.* Eusebius labeled these as *apocrypha* ("hidden"), *History of the Church,* 3:3.

[8]What Eusebius called *pseudepigrapha* ("false writings"). *History of the Church,* 6:12, citing Serapion of Antioch (ca 200).

[9]Councils at Hippo (393) and Carthage (397) formally ratified the Gospels as well as the remainder of the New Testament canon.

[10]Some scholars contend that the *Gospel of Thomas,* one of the "lost gospels" in question, has material that goes back to the 1st century, possibly containing traditions that pre-date Matthew, Mark and Luke. This issue is addressed later in Chapter Four. A few scholars also contend that the *Gospel of Peter* is independent of the canonical Gospels, and may predate them, but this view is fraught with problems. See Craig A. Evans, *Fabricating Jesus* (Downers Grove, Ill: InterVarsity, 2006), 78-85 for an excellent discussion. Otherwise, scholarly consensus considers no credible evidence for "lost gospels" that are earlier than the middle of the 2nd century.

[11]One probable exception is found in the *Egerton Gospel,* fragment 2, which seems to relate a miracle by Jesus in which he throws seed into the Jordan River that immediately bears fruit, to the delight of those standing by. The condition of the fragment leaves some room for doubt as to the details of this story.

[12]Bruce Metzger, *The Princeton Seminary Bulletin* 39, 1945, 12.

[13]*Acts of Paul* (ca 190). In this apocryphal work, after Paul baptizes the lion, he is later brought into the arena in Ephesus

to be devoured by wild beasts. A large lion is loosed to kill Paul, but to Paul's surprise it was the same lion he had previously baptized. The lion speaks to Paul, and, as Bruce Metzger once described it, "they escaped, walking out arm in paw." According to Tertullian, the *Acts of Paul* was written by a presbyter who wanted to honor Paul. The writing became very popular but was condemned by the Church, resulting in the presbyter's resigning his office. For a full treatment of Paul and the baptized lion, see Bruce Metzger, *The Princeton Seminary Bulletin* 39, 1945, 11-21.

[14]Against Heresies, 1.20.1.

[15]The oldest copy of the *Infancy Gospel of James* is an incomplete Greek manuscript dating to around ca 300, discovered in 1958, and is part of the Bodmer papyri (Papyrus Bodmer 5).

[16]So she pointed to him. They said, How can we speak to one who is in the cradle a child? [Jesus] said, Indeed, I am the servant of Allah. He has given me the Scripture and made me a prophet. And He has made me blessed wherever I am and has enjoined upon me prayer and zakah as long as I remain alive. And [made me] dutiful to my mother, and He has not made me a wretched tyrant. And peace is on me the day I was born and the day I will die and the day I am raised alive. That is Jesus, the son of Mary--the word of truth about which they are in dispute. Qur'an, Sura 19:29-34, Sahih International Translation.

[17]According to Eusebius, Hegesippus wrote five volumes called *Hypomnemata* ("Memoirs"). *Church History,* 2.23; 3.20; 3.32; 4.8; 4.22.

[18]Craig. A. Evans, *Fabricating Jesus* (Downers Grove, Ill: InterVarsity, 2006), 55.

[19]Evans, ibid, 54.

[20]Evans, ibid, 54.

[21]Evans, ibid, 54.

[22]Raymond E. Brown, "The Gnostic Gospels," *The New York Times Book Review,* 20 Jan. 1980, 3.

[23]Andrew Gregory, *The non-canonical gospels and the historical Jesus – some reflections on issues and methods,* Evangelical Quarterly, 81.1, 2009. 3-22.

[24]Bart Ehrman, *Lost Scriptures: Books that did not make it into the New Testament* (Oxford: Oxford Press, 2003), 19-20.

[25]Eusebius, *History of the Christian Church,* 3:25. Some scholars say it is not clear that Eusebius meant the *Gospel of Thomas* as opposed to other spurious works attributed to Thomas.

[26]Evans, ibid., 67.

[27]Evans, ibid., 67.

[28]Evans, ibid., 67.

[29]E.g., Stevan L. Davies, Elaine Pagels, Helmut Koester, Gilles Quispel, John Dominic Crossan, Robert W. Funk.

[30]Evans, ibid., 67-68. Evans gives a full treatment on pp. 68-77.

[31]*Against Heresies,* 1.31.1.

[32]H. H. Drake Williams III, *Jesus Tried and True* (Eugene, Oregon: Wipf & Stock, 2013), 119.

[33]Using carbon 14 plus Coptic paleography and orthography (study of ancient writing).

[34]Bart D. Ehrman, "Christianity Turned on its Head: The Alternate Vision of the Gospel of Judas," in *The Gospel of Judas,* K. Kasser, et al., ed. (Washington: National Geographic, 2006), 80.

[35]See April D. DeConick, *The Thirteen Apostle,* rev. ed (London: Continuum, 2009), and S. Gathercole, "The Gospel of Judas" in *The Non-Canonical Gospels,* P. Foster, ed. (London: T&T Clark, 2008), 84-95.

[36]The transcendent God of Sethian Gnosticism was known only to Jesus and the Gnostic elect. The Sethians trace their roots to Seth, the third son of Adam and Eve.

[37]DeConick, ibid, 24.

[38]E.g., James Robinson, *From the Nag Hammadi Codices to the Gospel of Mary and the Gospel of Judas,* Institute for Antiquity and Christianity Occasional Papers 48 (Claremont, CA: Institute for Antiquity and Christianity), 2006.

[39]*Against Heresies*, 3.11.9.

[40]Docetism (from the Greek word *dokeo* that means "seem" or "appear"), was a 2nd century heresy that believed Jesus merely *appeared* to be truly human, but His human form was merely an illusion. Thus, Docetism denies the incarnation of Jesus (John 1:14, "The Word became flesh and dwelt among us").

[41]*History of the Church*, 3.25.6.

[42]Evans, ibid, 80-85.

[43]Helmut Koester, *Ancient Christian Gospels* (Harrisburg, PA: Trinity Press, 1990), 216-240.

[44]E.g., John P. Meier, *A Marginal Jew: Rethinking the Historical Jesus* (New York: Doubleday, 1991), 112-166.

[45]*Papyrus Berolinensis* 8502, also known as the Akhmim Codex. It contains the *Apocryphon of John*, the *Sophia of Jesus Christ* and a summary of the *Act of Peter*.

[46]Evans, ibid, 94.

[47]LXX stands for the *Septuagint,* the Greek translation of the Hebrew Old Testament, traditionally believed to be translated by 70 Jewish scholars, hence, it is designated by the Roman numeral LXX. The LXX may have been commissioned first as a translation of the Torah (Five Books of Moses) around 250 B.C. by Ptolemy II Philadelphus, King of Egypt, then expanded to include the entire *Tanach* (Old Testament), with a completion sometime around 130 B.C. The New Testament quotes the LXX in many places, especially in Paul's Epistles.

[48]*Gospel of Philip,* 55.23-24, "Some said 'Mary conceived by the Holy Spirit.' They are in error. They do not know what they are saying."

[49]Helmut Koester and John Dominick Crossan argue that the *Egerton Gospel,* consisting of four fragments that contain parallels to canonical Gospel stories, represents a tradition that predates the canonical Gospels. As Craig Evans points out, there are elements (e.g., a fanciful story) that look like 2nd century or later non-canonical gospels. Evans, ibid., 86-92.

[50]The *Secret Gospel of Mark* appears to be a 20th century forgery. See Evans, ibid, 94-97 for a full treatment.

[51]*Pistis Sophia* is a Gnostic text originally written around the year 200. It presents Jesus as remaining on earth 11 years after His resurrection rather than the 40 days stated in the canonical *Book of Acts. Sophia* is the female deity of Gnosticism, and is identified in *Pistis Sophia* as the Holy Spirit.

[52]In college a skeptic told me that the canonical Gospels did not tell the whole story of Jesus, and if I wanted the full picture (which the skeptic said had been suppressed by the Church) I needed to read the *Aquarian Gospel.* My investigation revealed that the *Aquarian Gospel of Jesus the Christ* was written by Levi Dowling and was published in 1911. Dowling believed that through meditation he could explore the past and connect with "Akashic Records, the imperishable records of life preserved in the Supreme Intelligence or Universal Mind." As Dowling lay awake on the outskirts of Los Angeles, California between the hours of 2 and 6 a.m., he claims to have received emanations from beyond, and recorded them as the *Aquarian Gospel of Jesus the Christ.* Most of this gospel is about the "hidden years" of Jesus' youth, and some of the contents are derived from the pseudepigraphical *Gospel of James.*

[53]For further study, see Edgar J. Goodspeed, *Famous Biblical Hoaxes, or, Modern Apocryhpa* (Grand Rapids: Baker, 1956).

## CHAPTER FIVE
## ENDNOTES

[1]Michael Baigent, Richard Leigh and Henry Lincoln, *Holy Blood, Holy Grail* (London: Jonathan Cape, 1982), 389-90.

[2]Bruce Metzger, *The Text of the New Testament* (Oxford:1968), Preface v.

[3]See Metzger, ibid, pp. 207-212 for a list of the canons.

[4]New Testament textual criticism examines Greek manuscripts, versions (translations of the New Testament or portions thereof from Greek in other languages, such as Latin) and citations from post-apostolic Church Fathers to reconstruct the text.

[5]A term I created to replace the term "bibliographical test" originally coined by Chauncy Sanders to detect manuscript forgeries and not to determine the fidelity of textual transmission as commonly used by Christian apologists. See Chauncey Sanders, *An Introduction to Research in English Literary History* (New York, MacMillan, 1952), 143ff.

[6]The Institute for New Testament Textual Research, https://www.uni-muenster.de/INTF/KgLSGII2010_02_04.pdf. Accessed September 21, 2016.

[7]Josh McDowell & Clay Jones, *The Bibliographical Test*, updated 8-13-14, http://ibs.cru.org/files/6314/2108/7768/Bibliographical_Test_Josh_McDowell.pdf, adapted from Clay Jones, "The Bibliographical Test Updated," Christian Research Journal, vol. 35, no. 3, 2012. Accessed September 10, 2015.

[8]E.g., P[46], which this author has viewed in the Chester Beatty Library in Dublin, Ireland. P[46] contains complete copies of many of Paul's letters and was copied around the year A.D. 200, or perhaps earlier.

[9]Westcott and Hort conclude that after careful textual analysis, the amount of the New Testament subject to doubt is perhaps 1/1,000th of the whole New Testament. Brooke Foss

Westcott and Fenton John Anthony Hort, *The New Testament in the Original Greek* (Cambridge and London, 1881), 565.

[10]F. F. Bruce, *The New Testament Documents—Are They Reliable?* (Grand Rapids: Eerdmans, 5th ed., 1960), 19.

[11]Frederic G. Kenyon, *The Bible and Archaeology* (New York: Harper and Row, 1940), 288-289.

[12]Bart D. Ehrman, *The Textual Reliability of the New Testament: Bart D. Ehrman and Daniel B. Wallace in Dialogue*, Robert B. Stewart, ed. (Minneapolis: Fortress, 2011), 19.

[13]Ferdinand Christian Baur, *Kritische Untersuchungen über die kanonischen Evangelien* (Tübingen: Verlag und Druck, 1847), 239.

[14]The possible exception being the ending to Mark's Gospel (16:9-20) which some scholars, including evangelicals such as Tom Wright, say was probably lost.

[15]John Warwick Montgomery, *History, Law and Christianity* (Irvine: NRP Books, 2014), 13.

[16]Textual critic Daniel B. Wallace appropriately makes a distinction between variations, categorizing them as (1) spelling changes or nonsense readings, (2) changes that cannot be translated and synonyms, (3) meaningful variations that are not "viable" (i.e., no reasonable argument for the variation being the original wording), and (4) variations that are meaningful *and* viable. This last category comprises "less than 1% of all textual variants." *Revisiting the Corruption of the New Testament* (Grand Rapids: Kregel, 2011), 40.

[17]Brooke Foss Westcott and Fenton John Anthony Hort, *The New Testament in the Original Greek* (Cambridge and London, 1881), 565.

[18]Daniel B. Wallace, J. Ed Komoszewski and M. James Sawyer, *Reinventing Jesus* (Grand Rapids: Kregel, 2006), 105.

[19]Bart D. Ehrman, *The Bart Ehrman Blog, "Ruffling the Feathers of My Fellow Textual Critics,"* ehrmanblog.org, accessed September 10, 2015.

[20]Bart D. Ehrman, *Misquoting Jesus: The Story Behind Who Changed the Bible and Why* (New York: Harper/Collins, 2007), appendix.

[21]Ravi Zacharias, *Can Man Live Without God* (Dallas: Word Publishing, 1994), 162.

## CHAPTER SIX
## END NOTES

[1]Aristotle, in *The Art of Poetry* 1460b-1461b, suggests that readers of poetry who find contradictions may have misunderstood the writer, or failed to consider ways to reconcile what is thought to be an error. The point Aristotle makes might loosely be referred to as giving the "benefit of the doubt" to the writer. Aristotle's argument has been morphed into a "dictum" by Christian apologists, that says, "the benefit of the doubt is to be given to the document itself, not arrogated by the critic to himself" (e.g., see John Warwick Montgomery, *History, Law and Christianity* (Irvine, California: NRP Books, 2014), 13).

Although I personally cannot find an instance in which Aristotle ever stated such a "dictum," the kernels of a "benefit of the doubt" principle may be gleaned from Aristotle's *The Art of Poetry.* Augustine followed an approach similar to Aristotle's: "For I confess to your Charity that I have learned to yield this respect and honor only to the canonical books of Scripture: of these alone do I most firmly believe that the authors were completely free from error. And if in these writings, I am perplexed by anything that appears to me opposed to truth, I do not hesitate to suppose that either the manuscript is faulty, or the translator has not caught the meaning of what was said, or I myself have failed to understand it" (Augustine, *Letter to Jerome,* 82.1).

[2]*Annals,* 15.44.

[3]*Jewish Wars,* 5.451.

[4]Vasilius Tzaferis, "Jewish Tombs At and Near Giv'at ha-Mivtar," *Israel Explorations Journal* 20 (1970), 38-59. See also

"The Crucifixion Website," http://www.the-crucifixion.org/cross.html.

[5]*Annals*, 15.44.

[6]Matthew 4:13, Luke 4:16.

[7]Archaeologist Yardenna Alexandre stated, "The discovery is of the utmost importance since it reveals for the very first time a house from the Jewish village of Nazareth and thereby sheds light on the way of life at the time of Jesus." Cited in Israel Antiquities Authority, "For the Very First Time: A Residential Building from the Time of Jesus was Exposed in the Heart of Nazareth," December 21, 2009. Some critics question Alexandre's conclusions, citing lack of peer review of her claims.

[8]Called "mythicists," the most well-known contemporary writers who deny Jesus existed are historian Richard Carrier, theologian Robert Price, Dominican Priest Thomas Brodie and George Albert Wells, a professor of German.

[9]John E. Remsberg, *The Christ: A Critical Review and Analysis of the Evidence* (Amherst, New York: Prometheus Books, 1994), originally published 1909. For a critique of Remsberg, see the chapter "Refuting 'Remsberg's List'" in James Patrick Holding, *Shattering the Christ Myth* (XulonPress, 2008), 89-94.

[10]Remsberg, ibid., cited in James D. Agresti, *Rational Conclusions* (Documentary Press, 2009), 17.

[11]The 1994 comedy starring Tom Hanks, based on the 1986 novel *Forrest Gump* by Winston Groom.

[12]Agresti, ibid., 17-18.

[13]Lous H. Feldman, *Josephus and Modern Scholarship* (Berlin and New York: de Gruyter, 1984), 684.

[14]E.g., see John P. Meier, *A Marginal Jew: Rethinking the Historical Jesus,* vol. 1 (New York: Yale University Press, 1991).

[15]Sanhedrin (Greek συνεδρα "sit together") was the Jewish Supreme Court that met daily in the Temple except Sabbaths and holy days to administer religious and civil justice within the scope of what the Roman occupiers allowed.

[16]Feldman, ibid., 705.

[17]Richard Bauckham, "For What Offense Was James Put to Death?" in *James the Just and Christian Origins,* Bruce David Chilton and Craig A. Evans, eds. (Boston: Brill, 1999), 199; see also Robert E. Van Voorst, *Jesus Outside the New Testament* (Grand Rapids: Eerdmans, 2000), 83; for a summary of many scholars' views, see Louis H. Feldman, *Josephus and Modern Scholarship (1937-1980)* (Berlin and New York: de Gruyter, 1984), 704-707.

[18]James Charlesworth, *Jesus Within Judaism* (Garden City: Doubleday, 1988), 96-97.

[19]Ronald Mellor, *The Roman Historians* (Routledge, 1999), 76.

[20]Mythicist George A. Wells argues that Tacitus' use of the title "procurator" for Pilate shows that Tacitus did not consult archives of Pilate's era, since "procurator" was used only during the second half of the 1st century, whereas the archives would have shown the correct title "prefect" for Pilate's era. Wells, *The Historical Evidence for Jesus* (Amherst: Prometheus Books, 1982), 16. However, several facts refute Wells's argument. For example, Philo, the Jewish writer from Alexandria who was a contemporary of Pilate, says Pilate was "one of the prefects appointed procurator of Judea." A. H. M. Jones, *Studies in the Roman Government and Law* (Barns and Noble, 1968), 115-125. For additional facts refuting Wells, see Agresti, ibid., 6-7.

[21]*Annals,* 3.19.

[22]For an extensive treatment of Tacitus' reference to Jesus, see James D. Agresti, *Rational Conclusions* (Documentary Press, 2009), 4-12.

[23]Some scholars believe the letter was written much later, perhaps near the end of the 3rd century, and is therefore not a significant early witness to Jesus and His crucifixion.

[24]See Robert E. Van Voorst, ibid; also Andreas J. Köstenberger, L. Scott Kellum and Charles L. Quarles, *The Cradle, the Cross, and the Crown: An Introduction to the New Testament* (Nashville: B&H Publishing Group, 2009).

[25]In Greek αξιοσ γαρ ο εργατησ του μισθου αυτου.

[26]There are two references to the principle Jesus states in Luke 10:7 ("the laborer is worthy of his wages") and which Paul quotes directly in 1 Timothy 5:18. These are Leviticus 19:13 and Deuteronomy 24:15, but the Septuagint text (Greek translation of the Old Testament) of these verses is totally different from what Luke and Paul write, meaning that Paul's quote does not come from the Old Testament, but from Luke 10:7.

[27]*First Epistle of Clement to the Corinthians,* chapters 13: "being especially mindful of the words of the Lord Jesus which He spoke, teaching us meekness and long-suffering. For thus He spoke: 'Be ye merciful, that ye may obtain mercy; forgive, that it may be forgiven to you; as ye do, so shall it be done unto you; as ye judge, so shall ye be judged; as ye are kind, so shall kindness be shown to you; with what measure ye mete, with the same it shall be measured to you.'" And chapter 46 ("Remember the words of our Lord Jesus Christ, how He said, "Woe to that man [by whom offenses come]....")

[28]Ignatius' *Epistle to the Smyrnaens,* chapter 3: "When, for instance, He came to those who were with Peter, He said to them, 'Lay hold, handle Me, and see that I am not an incorporeal spirit.'" Cf. Luke 24:39.

[29]Polycarp's *Epistle to the Philippians,* 2:3 and 7:2.

[30]The medical term is *spondylolisthesis,* a defect in the bony prominence (*pars interarticularis*) of a vertebra, usually in the lumbar spine, typically L4, when one vertebra slides down onto the vertebra below it. Approximately 6% of the population has the condition, and most do not have any symptoms.

[31]The medical term is *asymptomatic,* meaning "without pain" or "without symptoms."

[32]Despite Jesus' claims that He was going to rise from the dead, and despite eyewitness testimony from the other 10 disciples that after His crucifixion Jesus appeared to them alive, the Apostle Thoma, refused to believe that Jesus had risen.

Thomas wanted empirical evidence, i.e., he wanted to see and touch Jesus to verify it was really Him (John 20:25) before he would believe. When Jesus later appeared to the disciples with Thomas present, upon seeing Jesus Thomas made his great confession, "My Lord and my God" (John 20:28). There is no evidence that Thomas touched Jesus before he made the confession (John 20:29, Jesus said, "because you have *seen* Me, have you believed?"). It appears that Thomas slightly lowered the evidentiary bar from the pre-conditions he first demanded before he would believe that Jesus rose.

[33]C. Stephen Evans, "The Historical Reliability of John's Gospel: From What Perspective Should It Be Assessed? in *The Gospel of John and Christian Theology,* Richard Bauckham and Carl Mosser, eds. (Grand Rapids: Eerdmans, 2008), 92-93.

[34]Evans, ibid., 95.

[35]*History and Christianity* (Downers Grove, Illinois: InterVarsity, 1971), 40.

[36]Archibald M. Hunter, *Bible and Gospels* (Philadephia: Westminster, 1969), 32-27, cited in Gary Habermas, *The Historical Jesus* (Joplin, Missouri: College Press, 1999), 108.

[37]*Encyclopedia Britannica* 15 ed. 1974, p. 145.

[38]*The CASE for the Resurrection of JESUS* (Grand Rapids: Kregel, 2004), 127-128.

[39]*The New Testament: A Historical Introduction to the Early Christian Writings,* 2nd ed. (New York: Oxford University Press, 2000) 124.

[40]*The Historical Reliability of the Gospels,* 2nd ed. (Downers Grove, Illinois: InterVarsity, 2007), 320.

## CHAPTER SEVEN
## END NOTES

[1]Paul uses the Greek word *historesai* in Galatians 1:18, translated *"to get acquainted with* Peter." The root of this word, *histor,* is the basis for the English word *history. Historesai* has

the meaning of "inquire" as with an historian or investigative journalist trying to determine details of reported events.

[2]Ludemann, Gerd. *The Resurrection of Jesus.* Trans. John Bowden (Minneapolis, Minnesota: Fortress Press, 1994), 171-72.

[3]Dunn, James D. G. *Jesus Remembered.* (Grand Rapids: Eerdmans, 2003), 854-55.

# BIBLIOGRAPHY

Agresti, James D. *Rational Conclusions.* Documentary Press, 2009.

Arndt, William F. and F. Wilbur Gingrich. *A Greek-English Lexicon of the New Testament and Other Early Christian Literature,* 4th ed. Chicago: University of Chicago Press, 1952.

Atkinson, Richard & R. M. Shiffrin, "Human memory: A proposed system and its control processes" In *The Psychology of Learning and Motivation,* vol. 8 edited by K. W. Spence and J. T. Spence. London: Academic Press, 1968.

Baigent, Michael, Richard Leigh and Henry Lincoln. *Holy Blood, Holy Grail.* London: Jonathan Cape, 1982.

Bauckham, Richard. "For What Offense Was James Put to Death?" In *James the Just and Christian Origins,* Bruce David Chilton and Craig A. Evans, eds. Boston: Brill, 1999.

Baur, Ferdinand Christian. *Kritische Untersuchungen über die kanonischen Evangelien.* Tübingen: Verlag und Druck, 1847.

Beasely-Murray, George R. *John,* 2nd ed.; World Bible Commentary 36. Columbia: Thomas Nelson, 1999.

Blomberg, Craig L. *The Historical Reliability of John's Gospel.* Downers Grove: InterVarsity Press, 2001.

_____. *The Historical Reliability of the Gospels,* 2nd ed. Downers Grove: InterVarsity Press, 2007.

Bloom, Jim. *Josephus as a Source for a Military History of the Jewish Revolt.* An abridgment of an address to the military classics seminar, Fort Meyer, Virginia, September 19, 2000. http://www.josephus.org/FlJosephus2/bloomRevolt.htm

Bock, Darrell. *Luke 1:1-9:50,* Baker Exegetical Commentary on the New Testament. Grand Rapids: Baker, 1994, 18.

Breck, John. John 21: Appendix, Epilogue or Conclusion? *St. Vladimir's Theological Quarterly* 36, 1992, 27-49.

Brown, Raymond E. "The Gnostic Gospels," *The New York Times Book Review,* January 20, 1980, 3.

Brown, Roger and James Kulik. Flashbulb memories. *Cognition* 5 (1): 73–99, 1977.

Bruce, F. F. *The New Testament Documents Are They Reliable?* Grand Rapids: Eerdmans, 5th rev. ed., 1960.

Burridge, Richard. *What Are the Gospels? A Comparison with Graeco-Roman Biography.* Cambridge: Cambridge University Press, 1992.

Carson, D.A. and Douglas Moo. *An Introduction to the New Testament,* 2nd ed. Grand Rapids: Zondervan, 2005.

_____. *The Gospel According to John,* Pillar New Testament Commentary. Grand Rapids: Eerdmans, 1991.

Cassels, Walter Richard. *Supernatural Religion: An Inquiry,* 6th ed. Toronto and Detroit: Rose-Belford, 1879.

Charlesworth, James. *Jesus Within Judaism.* Garden City: Doubleday, 1988.

Craig, William Lane. "Gospel Authorship—Who Cares?" www.reasonablefaith.org/gospel-authorship-who-cares, Q & A with William Lane Craig #373, June 8, 2014, retrieved September 13, 2016.

Crossan, John Dominic. *Jesus: A Revolutionary Biography.* New York: Harper Collins, 1995.

Crossley, James. *The Date of Mark's Gospel: Insight from the Law in Earliest Christianity.* London: T&T Clark/Continuum, 2004.

De Bruyne, Dom Donatien. "Les plus anciens prologues latins des Evangiles," *Revue Benedictine,* XL, 1928.

DeConick, April D. *The Thirteenth Apostle: What the Gospel of Judas Really Says,* rev. ed. London: Continuum, 2009.

Derickson, Gary W. "Matthean Priority/Authorship and Evangelicalism's Boundary," *The Master's Seminary* Journal 14/1, Spring 2003, 87-103.

Dowling, Levi. *Aquarian Gospel of Jesus the Christ*, 1911.

Drobner, H. R. *The Fathers of the Church: A Comprehensive Introduction.* Peabody, Massachusetts: Hendrickson, 2007.

Dunn, James D. G. *Christology in the Making: A New Testament Inquiry into the Origins of the Doctrine of the Incarnation*, 2d ed. Grand Rapids: Eerdmans, 1996.

_____. *Jesus Remembered.* Grand Rapids: Eerdmans, 2003.

Ehrman, Bart D. *Christianity Turned on its Head: The Alternate Vision of the Gospel of Judas,"* in *The Gospel of Judas,* K. Kasser, et al., ed. Washington: National Geographic, 2006.

_____. *Forgery and Counterforgery: The Use of Literary Deceit in Early Christian Polemics.* Oxford Academic, 2012.

_____. *Jesus: Apocalyptic Prophet of the New Millennium.* Oxford: Oxford University Press, 1999.

_____. *Lost Scriptures: Books that did not make it into the New Testament.* Oxford: Oxford Press, 2003.

_____. *Misquoting Jesus: The Story Behind Who Changed the Bible and Why.* New York: Harper/Collins, 2007.

_____. *The Bart Ehrman Blog, "Ruffling the Feathers of My Fellow Textual Critics,"* ehrmanblog.org, accessed September 10, 2016.

_____. *The New Testament: A Historical Introduction to the Early Christian Writings,* 4th ed. Oxford: Oxford University Press, 2008.

_____ and Daniel B. Wallace. *The Textual Reliability of the New Testament: Bart D. Ehrman and Daniel B. Wallace in Dialogue,* Robert B. Stewart, ed. Minneapolis: Fortress, 2011, 19.

*Encyclopedia Britannica* 15th ed. 1974.

Evans, C. Stephen. "The Historical Reliability of John's Gospel: From What Perspective Should It Be Assessed? In *The Gospel of John and Christian Theology,* Richard Bauckham and Carl Mosser, eds. Grand Rapids: Eerdmans, 2008.

Evans, Craig A. *Fabricating Jesus*. Downers Grove: InterVarsity Press, 2006.

_____. *Luke*. Hendricksen: Peabody, 1990.

Feldman, Louis H. *Josephus and Modern Scholarship (1937-1980)*. Berlin and New York: de Gruyter, 1984.

_____. *Studies in Josephus' Rewritten Bible*. Brill: Leiden, 1998.

Ferguson, Matthew. "Why Scholars Doubt the Traditional Authors of the Gospels," https://celsus.blog/2013/12/17/why-scholars-doubt-the-traditional-authors-of-the-gospels/ posted December 17, 2013, retrieved September 16, 2016.

Fisher, David Hackett. *Historian's Fallacies: Toward a Logic of Historical Thought*. New York: Harper and Row, 1970.

Fitzmeyer, J.A. *The Gospel According to Luke* (I-IX). Anchor Bible, 28. Garden City, NY: Doubleday, 1981, 1:53-57.

France, R. T. *The Gospel of Mark*, New International Greek Testament Commentary. Grand Rapids: Eerdmans, 2002.

Funk, Robert W. *Honest to Jesus: Jesus for a New Millennium*. San Francisco: Harper, 1996.

_____, Roy W. Hoover, and the Jesus Seminar. *The Five Gospels: What Did Jesus Really Say?* New York: MacMillan, 1993.

Gathercole, S. "The Gospel of Judas" *The Non-Canonical Gospels,* ed. P. Foster. London: T & T Clark, 2008, 84-95.

Goodspeed, Edgar J. *Famous Biblical Hoaxes, or, Modern Apocrypha*. Grand Rapids: Baker, 1956.

Green, Peter. *Alexander of Macedon, 356-323 B.C.: A Historical Biography*. University of California Press, 1992.

Gregory, Andrew. *The Non-Canonical Gospels and the Historical Jesus – Some Reflections on Issues and Methods,* Evangelical Quarterly, 81.1, 2009, 3-22.

Guthrie, Donald. *New Testament Introduction*, 3d ed. rev. Downers Grove: InterVarsity, 1970.

Gutwenger, Engelbert. *The Anti-Marcionite Prologues*, cdn. theologicalstudies.net, retrieved June 26, 2016.

Habermas, Gary and Michael Licona. *The CASE for the Resurrection of JESUS*. Grand Rapids: Kregel, 2004.

_____. *The Historical Jesus*. Joplin, Missouri: College Press, 1999.

_____. "Recent Perspectives on the Reliability of the Gospels," *Christian Research Journal*, vol. 28, number 1, 2005.

Harnack, Adoph. *The Oxford Dictionary of the Christian Church*, edited by F. L. Cross. New York: Oxford University Press, 2005.

_____. "Die altesten Evangelien-Prologe und die Bildung des Neuen Testaments." Sitzungsberichte der Preuss, Akademie der Wissenschaften, phil-hist Klasse, XXIV, 1928.

Harris, Murray J. *Raised Immortal: Resurrection and Immortality in the New Testament*. Grand Rapids: Eerdmans, 1985.

Hemer, Colin J. *The Book of Acts in the Setting of Hellenistic History*, edited by C. H. Gempf. Tübingen: Mohr, 1989.

Hendriksen, William. *Exposition of the Gospel According to John*. New Testament Commentary. Grand Rapids: Baker, 1953.

Hengel, Martin. *Acts and the History of Earliest Christianity*. Philadelphia: Fortress, 1980.

Hill, C.E. *The Johannine Corpus in the Early Church*. Oxford: Oxford University Press, 2004.

Holding, James Patrick. *Shattering the Christ Myth*. XulonPress, 2008.

Hunter, Archibald M. *Bible and Gospels*. Philadephia: Westminster, 1969.

Israel Antiquities Authority, "For the Very First Time: A Residential Building from the Time of Jesus was Exposed in the Heart of Nazareth," December 21, 2009.

Jones, A.H.M. *Studies in the Roman Government and Law.* Barns and Noble, 1968.

Jones, Clay. The Bibliographical Test Updated. *Christian Research Journal,* vol. 35, no. 3, 2012.

Keener, Craig S. *A Commentary on the Gospel of Matthew.* Grand Rapids: Eerdmans, 1999.

_____. *Miracles: The Credibility of the New Testament Accounts,* two vols. Grand Rapids: Baker Academic, 2011.

Kensinger, Elizabeth A. *Remembering the Details: Effects of Emotion,* [Emot. Rev. 1, 99–113. 10.1177/1754073908100432], 2009.

Kenyon, Frederic G. *The Bible and Archaeology.* New York: Harper and Row, 1940.

Kilpatrick, G.D. *The Origins of the Gospel According to St. Matthew.* 1946.

Koester, Helmut. *Ancient Christian Gospels.* Harrisburg, PA: Trinity Press, 1990.

Köstenberger, Andreas J. *John.* Baker Exegetical Commentary on the New Testament, 2001b: 17-47. Grand Rapids: Baker Publishing Group, 2004.

_____, L. Scott Kellum and Charles L. Quarles. *The Cradle, the Cross, and the Crown: An Introduction to the New Testament.* Nashville: B&H Publishing Group, 2009.

Kruger, Michael. *The Question of Canon.* Downers Grove: InterVarsity Press, 2013.

Kümmel, W. G. *The New Testament: The History of the Investigation of Its Problems.* New York: Abingdon, 1970.

Licona, Michael R. *Why Are There Differences in the Gospels?* Oxford University Press, 2017.

Lightfoot, J.B. *The Apostolic Fathers.* MacMillan & Co. 1891.

_____. *Supernatural Religion,* 2nd ed. London: MacMillan & Co., 1889.

Lüdemann, Gerd. *What Really Happened to Jesus?* Trans. John Bowden. Louisville, Kentucky: John Knox Press, 1995.

_____. *The Resurrection of Jesus.* Trans. John Bowden. Minneapolis, Minnesota: Fortress Press, 1994.

Mather, Mara and Laura L. Carstensen. "Aging and motivated cognition: The positivity effect in attention and memory." *Trends in Cognitive Sciences,* Vol 9, Issue 10, October 2005, 496-502.

MacDonald, Dennis R. *Homeric Epics and the Gospel of Mark.* New Haven: Yale University Press, 2000.

Meier, John P. *A Marginal Jew: Rethinking the Historical Jesus,* vol. 1. New York: Yale University Press, 1991.

Mellor, Ronald. *The Roman Historians.* Routledge, 1999.

Metzger, Bruce M. *A Textual Commentary on the Greek New Testament.* London: United Bible Societies, 1971.

_____. *Literary Forgeries and Canonical Pseudepigrapha,* Journal of Biblical Literature, vol. 91, No. 1, March 1972, 3-24.

_____. *The Princeton Seminary Bulletin 39,* 1945, 11-21.

_____. *The Text of the New Testament,* Oxford:1968.

Montgomery, John Warwick. *History and Christianity.* Downers Grove: InterVarsity, 1971.

_____. *History, Law and Christianity.* Irvine, California: NRP Books, 2014.

Morris, Leon. *The Gospel According to John.* Grand Rapids, Eerdmans, 1971.

Pardee, Nancy. *The Genre of the Didache: A Text-Linguistic Analysis.* Dissertation, University of Chicago, 2002.

Qur'an, Sura 19:29-34, Sahih International Translation.

Raaijmakers, J. G. & Richard Shiffrin, "SAM: A theory of probabilistic search of associative memory" *The Psychology of Learning and Motivation,* edited by G. H. Bower, vol. 14, 207-262. New York: Academic Press, 1980.

Ramsay, Sir William. *St. Paul the Traveller and the Roman Citizen.* London: Hodder & Stroughton, 1925.

Remsberg, John E. *The Christ: A Critical Review and Analysis of the Evidence.* Amherst, New York: Prometheus Books, 1994 (originally published 1909).

Riesner, Ranier. *Paul's Early Period: Chronology, Mission Strategy, Theology.* Grand Rapids: Eerdmans, 1998.

Robinson, James. *From the Nag Hammadi Codices to the Gospel of Mary and the Gospel of Judas,* Institute for Antiquity and Christianity Occasional Papers 48. Claremont, CA: Institute for Antiquity and Christianity, 2006.

Robinson, John A. T. *Redating the New Testament.* Philadelphia: Westminster, 1976.

Sanders, Chauncey. *An Introduction to Research in English Literary History.* New York, MacMillan, 1952.

Scholtz, Donald. *Jesus in the Gospels and Acts: Introducing the New Testament.* Saint Mary's Press, 2009.

Schweitzer, Albert. *The Quest of the Historical Jesus,* published in German in 1913 as *Geschichte der Leben-Jesu-Forschung* and in English as *The Quest of the Historical Jesus,* trans. John Bowden, et al. 2nd ed. Minneapolis: Fortress Press, 2001.

Stein, Robert H. *Mark,* Evangelical Commentary of the New Testament. Grand Rapids: Baker, 2008, 12-15.

Stewart, John. *Inspiration.* JohnMarkStewartblogspot.com, February 10, 2010.

Tuckett, C.M. "The Didache." *The Reception of the New Testament in the Apostolic Fathers,* edited by A.F. Gregory and C.M. Tuckett. Oxford: Oxford University Press, 2005.

Tzaferis, Vasilius. "Jewish Tombs At and Near Giv'at ha-Mivtar," *Israel Explorations Journal* 20, 1970, 38-59.

Van Voorst, Robert E. *Jesus Outside the New Testament*. Grand Rapids: Eerdmans, 2000.

Wallace, Daniel B. *Greek Grammar Beyond the Basics*. Grand Rapids: Eerdmans, 1996), 531.

_____. *Matthew: Introduction, Argument, and Outline*, from series "New Testament Introductions and Outlines," bible.org, retrieved Sept. 7, 2016.

_____, J. Ed Komoszewski and M. James Sawyer, *Reinventing Jesus*. Grand Rapids: Kregel, 2006.

_____. *Revisiting the Corruption of the New Testament*, edited by Daniel B. Wallace. Grand Rapids: Kregel, 2011.

_____. *The Gospel of John: Introduction, Argument, Outline*, from series "New Testament Introductions and Outlines," bible.org, retrieved Sept. 7, 2016.

Wells, George A. *The Historical Evidence for Jesus*. Amherst: Prometheus Books, 1982.

Westcott, Brooke Foss and Fenton John Anthony Hort. *The New Testament in the Original Greek*. Cambridge and London, 1881.

Whately, Richard. *Historical Doubts Relative to Napoleon Bonaparte*. Public domain, 1818.

Williams III, H.H. Drake. *Jesus Tried and True*. Eugene, Oregon: Wipf & Stock, 2013.

Zacharias, Ravi. *Can Man Live Without God*. Dallas: Word Publishing, 1994.

86866791R00102

Made in the USA
Columbia, SC
06 January 2018

Christianity stands or falls on whether the Gospel accounts of the life, death and resurrection of Jesus are true. Are the accounts reliable? What is the evidence?

Most people have heard of the Gospels—Matthew, Mark, Luke, and John—writings that tell about the life and teachings of Jesus of Nazareth. Some people see the Gospels as true accounts of what Jesus said and did, while others see them as religious fiction. Lawyer and Christian Apologist John Stewart examines the question of whether the Gospels are reliable accounts of Jesus by investigating the six main questions people have about the Gospels:

- Were the Gospel accounts written when eyewitnesses were alive?
- Who wrote the Gospels—are the authors anonymous, or known?
- Does the evidence show the Gospel writers were honest or biased?
- Are there "Lost Gospels" that were intentionally kept out of the Bible?
- Has the content of the Gospels changed from the original wording?
- Do history and archaeology confirm the reliability of Gospel accounts?

John Stewart is a lawyer, Christian apologist and award-winning radio personality. He is the co-founder of Intelligent Faith and serves as Scholar in Residence for Ratio Christi, a student-faculty apologetics alliance. John holds a Masters' Degree in theological studies from Talbot School of Theology and a Doctorate in Jurisprudence from Western State College of Law. He is the author of five books, and has taught on the evidence for Christianity ("apologetics") for over 30 years in more than a dozen countries in North America, Asia and Africa. John has appeared on numerous radio and television programs around the world and frequently lectures and debates on university campuses. He is a visiting scholar at Multnomah Biblical Seminary in Portland, Oregon and his blogs appear at www. IntelligentFaith.com and JohnMarkStewart.blogspot.com.

ISBN 9781983584862

90000 >

9 781983 584862